GIRL
Unmasked

GIRL
Unmasked

How Uncovering
My Autism
Saved My Life

EMILY KATY

monoray

First published in Great Britain in 2024 by Monoray, an imprint of
Octopus Publishing Group Ltd
Carmelite House
50 Victoria Embankment
London EC4Y 0DZ
www.octopusbooks.co.uk

An Hachette UK Company
www.hachette.co.uk

ISBN (hardback): 978-1-80096-139-5
ISBN (trade paperback): 978-1-80096-140-1

A CIP catalogue record for this book is available from the British Library.

Printed and bound in Great Britain

Typeset in 11.5/15pt Cardo by Jouve (UK), Milton Keynes

10 9 8 7 6 5 4 3 2

This FSC® label means that materials used
for the product have been responsibly sourced

MIX
Paper | Supporting
responsible forestry
FSC
www.fsc.org
FSC® C104740

This monoray book was crafted and published by Jake Lingwood,
Pauline Bache, Monica Hope, Rachael Shone and Allison Gonsalves

For my mum and dad,
who never stopped fighting for me,
even when I couldn't fight for myself.

CONTENT WARNING

This book contains themes of self-harm, suicide, institutional harm and filicide. Suicide and self-harm methods are not specified, but some readers may find the themes upsetting nonetheless.

CONTENTS

AUTHOR'S NOTE I

This book tells my story truthfully. I have written it as accurately as I can remember it. However, there are periods on my journey where my memories are blurred so I have filled in the gaps in order to make sense of the narrative. It was also important to me to protect the privacy of other people. Hence, all names apart from those of close family members and a number of places have been changed. Likewise, I have altered identifying details of stories involving people other than my family or friends. In some cases, I have combined multiple storylines in order to make the book more readable; and in one instance, right at the very end of the book, I have created an imagined situation – in many ways a vision of my future. Wherever and whenever I have diverted from 100 per cent cold, hard facts, my thoughts and responses to the situation being illustrated remain very much true.

AUTHOR'S NOTE II

I love lists. And while it is a cliché that autistic people love lists, in my case it does happen to be true. However, I thought a list about why lists are great might go some way to explaining my thinking.

WHY LISTS ARE GREAT

» You can read one point at a time, so your brain doesn't get crowded.
» It is a very simple structure to follow, so you don't get confused.
» Lists are the opposite of chaotic.
» They are ordered, and order is great.
» You can make a list about absolutely anything.
» You can use lists to remember some very interesting things.
» They make things much easier to understand.
» They are quite satisfying to look at.

Warning: this book may contain a lot of lists. I would apologise to those who are not list-lovers, but I'm trying to stop apologising for being who I am.

INTRODUCTION

I never set out to write a memoir. I never saw myself as a very interesting person. I was never the child or teenager who everybody wanted to know. I was always late to the fashion trends, often barely managing to keep up at all. I was not funny, at least not in the way other children appreciated. At school, I wasn't interested in sports or music. Yes, my extracurricular activities did include netball and flute for a while, but only as a result of peer pressure and wanting to please my parents.

The thing I was interested in was books. And while *I* think that makes me a very interesting person, it did not help my popularity status at school. I had a core group of likeminded friends and tried to get through it all by ignoring everyone else. For the first chapter of my life, before the teenage desire to be liked really kicked in, I spent my days absorbed in other people's stories and writing my own. Writing has been a coping mechanism of mine for as long as I have been able to write.

I suppose that is how I found myself staring at pages after pages of my words, forming what appeared to be a memoir. I didn't feel the need to tell the world about myself as such. (After all, I am not very interesting.) But it transpired that I was unable to get across what I wanted to say without telling the world about myself in the process.

And there were a *lot* of things that I needed to tell the world. Because I felt like I had been failed, to some extent. And the more I found out that others were being failed too, the angrier and sadder I became. I couldn't just leave that be. I am the sort of person for whom that would be impossible.

I should introduce myself. My name is Emily. I am 22 years old. I don't *feel* 22. That sounds to me like a proper adult – though I have been told there is no such thing. I thought, by this age, I would have adjusted to adult life, been able to confidently engage in adult tasks and outgrown the needs I had when I was younger. It turns out, hitting 18 doesn't mean those needs magically go away. I'm sure this is the case for everyone. But when you're atypical, like me, adult life seems even harder to grasp.

Just over five years ago, when I was 16 years and 10 months old, I was diagnosed with autism. A diagnosis that I could barely comprehend at the time, but which has since allowed me to see my whole life with a clarity I had never had before.

A great deal of *stuff* had led to that moment. A lot of challenges, trauma and mistakes – but also joy, let's never forget the joy. Ever since I can remember, I have always felt different; and I always felt that that was a bad thing. I tried desperately to fit in, squeezing myself into the moulds that society had laid out for my life, and often found myself failing. As a result, I grew to believe that life wasn't for me, and that it never could be. This belief led me to some very dark places. Places from which my family and I, at times, thought I would never escape.

When I think back over my journey, I do feel sad for my younger self. But what I feel even more sad about is that I know there are so many others who have experienced similar journeys, and many who will do so in the future. A monumental number of autistic people reach rock bottom before finding out they are autistic, if they even get to find out at all. I was lucky that I did at the age I did, because there are many finding out much later in life, which may increase their risk of having poor mental health and a lower quality of life.[1] So many of us fly under the radar – invisible, unheard, unseen and unsupported. And because of the way that autism has been historically (mis)understood, this is particularly true for autistic women[2] and those assigned female at birth, as well as autistic people of colour.[3]

I want to make clear, though, that the journey of an autistic person who was diagnosed at an early age will not necessarily have been easier. Although it has the potential to, a diagnosis does not automatically lead to understanding and support, so it is not everything. Those diagnosed younger may have been forced into harmful therapies or institutions, learned to view autism as something inherently 'bad' or 'wrong' with them, and grown up experiencing just as many challenges. Likewise, somebody diagnosed later may have been well supported in their home and school environment, and had their needs catered for, just without a diagnosis.

What autistic people really need is a world that recognises us earlier, but then supports us to build a positive self-identity, provides the right adjustments and support and helps us to thrive. Unfortunately, very few of us receive these things.

This means that so many of us grow up feeling confused and misunderstood. It feels as though everyone around us has been given an instruction manual on how to think, act and behave, and that we have missed out. As though everyone is speaking in a foreign language, understanding all these social rules and just moving through life effortlessly around us. Meanwhile, our own brains are in complete overdrive just trying to understand what we should be doing or saying to not stick out like a sore thumb. (Idioms like this often do not make sense to me – I mean, whenever my thumb has been sore, no one has been able to see it, but I want to try to appeal to a neurotypical audience here too, so needs must!)

I have spent my whole life studying neurotypical people. These are people who have the majority neurotype. A typical brain, if you like. As I grew up, by copying them, I learned to socialise following their patterns and their cues. I learned what to do in certain situations by following their lead. I observed closely and learned what would make other people laugh and what would make them scrunch up their nose in distaste (though, I soon learned, that copying what made someone laugh in one situation may translate to rudeness in another). But however much I 'masked' (more of which later), I knew quite early on that I was not like them.

I do not know whether my life would have been easier had I grown up knowing that I was autistic. But I do know that growing up *not* knowing left a lot of scars – both metaphorically and physically. This book is all about that. The joy and the pain of my childhood, and the discovery of who I am and what came after.

This book is for anyone who wants to know more about autism. It is for anyone and everyone who wants to try to understand what being autistic can be like – especially for an autistic person growing up undiagnosed. It is for autistic people who are desperate to see themselves; though I can't promise my experience will reflect yours, as this is just the story of one relatively privileged autistic girl.

That is important to remember. I am just one autistic person, who grew up in a reasonably middle-class family. Many would call me 'high-functioning' and while I, along with many others of varied levels of support needs, disagree with functioning labels, I recognise that I do not have a learning disability and I am not non-speaking. But this is just my story. All autistic people are different. We all have different needs, different challenges and different strengths. Where I talk about autism, I do so based on my own experiences, the experiences

I have heard from others, the generally accepted views among the autistic community and evidence from research studies. But my aim is *never* to speak for all autistic people.

What I do know, though, is that when I left my assessment armed with the new knowledge I had, I sought out autistic voices, desperate for some connection, some mutual understanding and some community. I found many wonderful autistic people on social media, in books and even some in real life. Discovering these autistic voices gave me comfort and the space to learn about myself in a way that advice from professionals could never provide. I hope that this book adds to them.

PROLOGUE

I am running, though I'm not sure where to. I just know I need to get away. Away from the noise and the anxiety. Somewhere safe. I don't know where that is but I know it's not here.

The school buildings are getting smaller and smaller behind me. If my thoughts were coherent, they would tell me to turn back. But they're not. They are jumbled, confused, tangled up with one another.

The anxiety inside me rises more and more by the second. My heart hammers against my chest, blood pounding through my veins. My lungs are struggling to keep up as my breathing quickens. I think I am going to throw up.

The road is to my left. Car tyres screech against the tarmac and engines roar, piercing my ears. I need it to be quiet. I can't see properly. Tears blur my vision, but I can make out the shape of trees in the distance. Tall columns of green, clustered together for protection. I dart towards them. To safety.

I don't know how long I've been running for, but I make it to the edge of the forest. There is no path here, so I wade my way through the bushes, thorns scratching at my skin. I see red appear on my hand; it drips to the floor, staining the leaves a warm crimson. I keep going. Pushing through trees. Kicking branches out of my way. Struggling to contain my sobs.

I burst through the trees into a clearing. Here the late-afternoon sun fights its way through the leaves, breaking onto the woodland floor. I come to a sharp halt. My legs don't feel in my control, but for a moment I stand there and stare at the sky. It is dimmer than when I last looked. I try to take deep breaths to calm down, but it doesn't work. My breathing quickens even more. Sobs wrack my body. Everything around me begins to spin. I can hear someone hyperventilating. It doesn't feel like the sound is coming from my body, but there is no one else around.

A twig snaps and I jolt upright again. I'm not safe here either.

So, once more, I run, my body ablaze with fear.

The next time I look up at the sky, it is dark. So dark that I try to open my eyes before realising that they are already open, a blanket of jet-black staring down at me.

I am confused. I have no idea what the time is. My phone is back at school, in my bag by my desk. I was in a French lesson, I think. I can't remember. My brain is too foggy.

I feel something hard underneath me and realise that I am curled up on the ground. My knees are drawn to my chest as if I were a foetus. The ice-cold air pierces through my blazer to my skin. I am shivering, or perhaps shaking; I'm not sure. I try to move, but my body is like stone beneath me. So, I scream. But the only response is the echo of my own desperate cries bouncing off the trees around me.

Then the sound of an owl hooting sends a shock of panic through my spine. School must have ended hours ago. I can't tell if it is five o-clock or midnight. Chunks of time are missing from my memory.

I am really scared.

I know I need to move. I need to get warm. Perhaps my body is numb from the winter air, and that's why I can't move. But I must. As I try to push myself up, I realise that my hands are cloaked in mud. It is not hard and filthy, as I would have expected, but soft, like slime. Briefly, my thoughts drift to the pot of pink slime on my desk at home. My friend and I had made it last weekend, taking over the kitchen table with glitter, glue and paint. Mum hadn't been impressed. *Mum*, I think. Where does she think I am?

With a deep breath, I roll onto my back and force myself into a sitting position. I grab my legs and drag them to my chest. It feels like moving solid rock. I press my hands on the ground, wincing in pain from the cuts, and heave myself up. Then I steady myself, praying I don't fall down again.

It is too dark to see a path. So, I hold my arms out ahead of me and use them to guide my way. The pumping of blood around my veins and the thumping of my heartbeat fills the silence.

Then I hear it. The chopping of the rotors. An earsplitting buzz. I look upwards and see a light in the sky. A helicopter is circling above. I wonder if it is looking for me.

I head in its direction, stumbling as I push past branch after branch, not caring as they graze my skin. The woodland gradually begins to thin out and I find myself in an open field. There is grass under my feet now, not mud. And the helicopter is hovering directly above me.

The darkness ahead of me is interrupted by flashing blue light. It is almost blinding. Strangers in uniform tumble towards me and grab me roughly. I feel my legs go to jelly beneath me as I crumple to the ground. My hands press against my ears, hard, to block out the sound of shouting and roaring rotors.

A familiar voice calls out not to touch me, but I don't know who it is. Then warm hands wrap around me, and I hear the soft voice of my mum. Nervously, I look up. She and my teacher are crouched in front of me, in thick winter coats to protect them from the icy cold. My teacher shrugs his off and places it gently over my shoulders.

'You're okay,' Mum says, through her own tears. She pulls me even closer, tighter, and I don't think she will ever let me go.

Tears roll down my cheeks. They must hit my tongue because a salty taste fills my mouth. The taste of fear. I don't understand how I ended up here.

'I'm sorry,' I whisper, hugging my knees tightly to my chest. 'I'm so sorry.'

CHAPTER ONE

'Imagination is the only weapon in the war against reality.'
—*Benjamin de Casseres (attributed)*

It is the middle of the Easter holidays and I am eight years old. I'm in a garden filled with roses, somewhere in the South of France. The glistening sun streams through the trees, creating shapes on the grass. I'm crouched behind a prickly tree, peeking through the branches as my little brother and sister run around the pool of swans, chanting my name.

'Princess Emily! Princess Emily!'

We are in Crystal Kingdom, a world I have spent hours meticulously crafting. I have maps designed of the kingdom, showing the route from the forests to the castle and beyond. Our characters all have backstories that I have written out and stuffed under my bed alongside several short stories of our battles. This world is as real to me as reality.

My sister, Princess Jessica, my brother, Prince Thomas, and I are bravely defending our kingdom from the Red Knights, an evil army trying to destroy us.

I hear Jessica shriek. Her curly blonde locks flop across her eyes, sea-blue like mine. 'Princess Emily! They're coming!'

I move into position at once. I am wearing my golden armour, sitting on a valiant white horse. The reins slide between the fingers of my left hand, and my right grips tightly onto my sword – a sword that has been passed down our family for generations. It's rumoured to have magic powers; powers strong enough to defeat the Red Knights. I hold it out in front of me, watching its silver blade dazzle in the sunlight.

Suddenly, the knights appear ahead, galloping towards us on great black horses, twice the size of ours. The sun illuminates their skin. There must be a dozen of them and they are bolting towards the three of us. We are small and fragile. But I don't feel nervous. Why would I? We are the heroes in our story.

'Charge!' I yell at my siblings. They tell their horses to go, and we bolt into a delicate canter. At once, the breeze flushes across my face, warm and gentle. Our horses gracefully move us into a line, me in the middle, positioned barely a metre in front. We gallop towards our enemies, confident in our ability to defeat them.

And sure enough, as we meet, knight after knight is slain. I imagine their bodies collapsing onto the ground then evaporating into the air, never to be seen again.

'Go, be free!' I whisper to their horses. Their dark eyes meet mine and they give a brief nod, almost as if to thank me for their freedom.

'Victory!' Thomas announces, punching the air with his fist. Jessica spins on the spot, delighted squeals escaping her rosy lips.

'Well done all,' I nod gravely, my demeanour making clear that it will not be the last we see of the Red Knights.

But, for now, they are defeated. And we are left unscathed. Another successful day in Crystal Kingdom.

'Emily! Thomas! Jessica!' A shout, unfamiliar to the world of Crystal Kingdom, interrupts our imaginations. 'Dinner!'

Three white swans appear, gracefully lifting us off our feet and up into the air. Up high, wind on our faces, we feel free. The sun is beginning to set on the horizon, the sky bursting with red and gold hues. The swans circle us around the kingdom to check that all is in order. It is. The turrets of our palace come into view and the villagers wave up at us from down below. They pull their shop shutters down, signalling the end of another day. Then another shout disturbs us, and we are plummeted back down to the ground. The world evaporates into dust.

Reluctantly, we leave Crystal Kingdom behind us and head inside the chalet for dinner. Mum has made spaghetti bolognese. I'm still overly excited by having slain the Red Knights and can't focus on the dinner-time conversation. I am impatient, far too eager to get back to the magic outside.

'I know you're excited but breathe! Let us talk too!' Mum chuckles, passing the garden salad across the table. I still do not like salad. Lettuce is too bland, too bitter. Tomatoes squelch uncomfortably in my mouth, without warning of whether they will be sweet or sour. The only thing I do like is cucumber. It is juicy and predictable. I reach over now and pick it out with my fingers still wrinkled from the pool water.

'Whoops, sorry,' I grin. I hadn't even realised sentences had been flooding out of me. I swallow hard, imagining a ball at the back of my throat stopping me from talking. My thoughts are desperate to escape and it takes energy to squash them.

'But you all had a good time. That's good to hear,' Dad says, helping Jessica to cut up her spaghetti. She already has sauce plastered all over her face. Thomas does too. They are only three and five, yet already make strong companions in fighting the Red Knights. It would help if Jessica could run a bit faster without falling over, but luckily our magic powers help us compensate for this.

After dinner, we rush back outside, leaving Mum and Dad washing up at the sink. The sky is now dimming, and the shade steals more of the sun each minute. Soon it is hard for us to see, but each time we are encouraged inside we beg for five more minutes. We don't have many evenings left; we want to make the most of them.

The rest of our holiday is filled with more adventures in Crystal Kingdom, hours spent splashing in the pool and devouring ice lolly after ice lolly. My favourites are Fruit Twisters, a perfect blend of pineapple ice cream and strawberry–lemon ice that melts satisfyingly on my tongue. Mum and Dad give us the freedom we desperately crave, to race around the gardens until dinnertime. When we have to go back to England, we are all sad. But no one more than me. For me, going home means fewer hours can be spent with the characters inside my head and more must be spent with those from whom I cannot escape.

In 1943, the Austrian-American psychiatrist Leo Kanner published a paper titled 'Autistic Disturbances of Affective Contact', in which he described eleven children who appeared to have similar characteristics. He suggested that they all exhibited the traits of 'extreme autistic aloneness', literalness, repetitive behaviour, differences in speech, and 'an anxiously obsessive desire for the maintenance of sameness'.[1] The following year, in 1944, he named this 'early infantile autism'.[2]

This contradicted how Eugen Bleuler, a German psychiatrist, had defined autism 32 years earlier. He had coined the term to explain a symptom of schizophrenia, describing withdrawal from reality by immersion into fantasy, or an 'inner life'.[3] But, by 1943, the term had been redefined.

Still, it took until 1977 for Michael Rutter and Susan Folstein at the Institute of Psychiatry, London, to conduct the first twin study,[4] a type of research that aims to disentangle the influence of the environment from genetics on a specific characteristic. Twin researchers compare the commonality of identical twins (who share 100 per cent of their genes) with non-identical twins (who share only 50 per cent) in relation to specific traits; a trait that is more prevalent in identical twins is likely to have a genetic basis. Rutter and Folstein studied 21 sets of identical and non-identical twins where at least one of each pair had autism. They found that 36 per cent of identical twins shared their diagnosis with their twin, whereas none of the non-identical twins did. These findings provided evidence for the genetic basis of autism for the first time. Alongside observing core autistic traits, Rutter and Folstein noted that many of the children appeared to have 'limited imagination' with 'no imaginative play'. In fact, Rutter had already claimed that 'the autistic child has a deficiency of fantasy rather than an excess'.[5]

Impaired imagination, alongside social interaction and communication, became what was labelled the 'triad of impairments'[6] – essential features of autism developed by Wing and Gould in 1979.[7] This idea of limited imagination in autistic people was observed and shared among many leading researchers and clinicians, including Wing,[8] and Craig and Baron–Cohen.[9]

And thus began the myth that would still prevail decades later: the idea that *all* autistic people lack imagination. Although Wing clarified in an interview in 2010 that 'autistic children do have imagination, but it is not social',[10] this idea was already popular in the autism field.

WHY PEOPLE THINK AUTISTIC PEOPLE LACK IMAGINATION

» Powerful people said so decades ago.
» Pretend play may look different in autistic children.*
  Some like to line up their toys or take them apart to see
  how they work; some like to play individually rather than
  with peers; and some are more influenced by reality
  than non-autistic children.
» Professionals still refuse to give a diagnosis based on the
  fact the child is too imaginative.
» Autistic people may find it harder to express what is
  going on inside their minds.
» Autistic people may find it harder to imagine
  hypothetical or unrealistic scenarios.
» Autistic people tend to pay strict attention to facts and
  detail.
» Autistic people may imagine individually rather than
  with others.
» Some autistic people may have aphantasia, meaning
  they are unable to visualise things, which may affect
  how they imagine.
» People tend to jump at any slight difference and call it a
  deficit.

---

* This is seen as a real cause for concern. I still haven't worked
out why. Autistic children's play is often criticised or framed as
a deficit because it is not always the same as their non-autistic
peers. But why not celebrate their differences and recognise their
strengths? One study suggests that autistic children play more
fairly with their peers than non-autistic children.[11] Another
suggests they are overly caring, loving and kind towards others.[12]
Yet we don't talk about that, do we?

» Some autistic people may not be imaginative, but this does not mean that all aren't.
» The difference between social imagination and creative imagination is not understood.

Now, don't get me wrong, some autistic people do have 'difficulties' with imagination. Though whether this is really a difficulty or just a difference will depend on the lens it is being seen through. These 'difficulties' may mean some autistic people don't find themselves in imaginary worlds the way that I did, because the literality of their brains doesn't enable this. Or, like Wing suggested,[13] it may mean that they have plenty of imaginary friends but struggle with *social imagination*. This is much more common.

Social imagination is often confused with a lack of creativity. But it is not the same as dreaming up faraway lands and having an imaginary friend (although this may be hard for some too). You see, social imagination refers to the ability to imagine and process things that we are not familiar with. For example, understanding abstract concepts, being able to cope in unfamiliar situations and being able to imagine an alternative outcome or routine to what we are used to.

The blanket myth that autistic people lack imagination is harmful. It is frequently heard to be a reason why autistic people are not given a diagnosis. Because their mind is able to construct some magnificent – and sometimes, horrific – things, they are told they can't be autistic. But that is *creative* imagination; and having creative imagination does not preclude struggles with *social* imagination.

So, considering that I spent most of my younger years embedded in a world of fiction, incredibly intense and real to me, the possibility of me being autistic was totally out of the question. I kept my head buried in stories, devouring a novel a day by the time I was eight. I dreamed up fantasy lands to escape to, my creative imagination vibrant, because the real world just seemed boring. I enjoyed pretend play, providing I was in control of the environment. If I was not, and my idea of how the play should go was changed to something I was unfamiliar with, I found this difficult to process (indicating my struggle with social imagination). The lines between reality and fantasy were often blurred in my mind and understanding that the world of fiction books was just that – fiction – was something my brain, wired to take things extremely literally, just did not understand.

These lines were so blurred that one drizzly afternoon, I convinced my little brother to run away with me so that we could begin our own adventure. I had read every single book from Enid Blyton's *The Famous Five* and *The Secret Seven* collections that I could get my hands on and thought that running away would kick-start my own adventure in saving kidnapped children and travelling across abandoned rail tracks to find criminals. Well, it was partly that and partly the fact that I had been unfairly told off earlier that day. At that age, my extremely strong sense of justice hadn't quite been appropriately reigned in. So, I packed a bag and asked my seven-year-old brother if he wanted to come along with me. He looked at me with glee and excitedly ran to pack his own backpack. With his little hand in mine, we slipped out of the front door when we thought no one was looking. Sadly, by the time we reached the end of the drive, a shout from the front door meant our fantasies were put to an abrupt halt. Which was probably for the best, considering I had no ability to fathom the danger I could have put us both in.

Mum and Dad were furious, of course. I don't think I quite managed to get them to understand the reasoning for my actions, which I still believed were entirely valid. They did inform me, though, that my packing was very thorough, and that I was very well-prepared, which I took as a compliment. Looking back, this may well have been sarcasm that went straight over my head. My punishment was no electronics for a week – no TV, no computer, no DS. This didn't bother me terribly. I just spent even longer reading and forcing my parents to endure board game after board game in the evenings, a weak attempt at entertaining myself. They were probably more relieved than I was when the week came to an end.

My attempt at running away may suggest otherwise, but it is fair to say that I had a pretty happy childhood. I lived in a nice house, I had nice things, I was safe and I was loved. I might not have said that to you back then though, judging by the stacks of diaries still stuffed at the back of my cupboard, where I regularly roasted my mother for telling me off and my brother for getting me into trouble. But the imagination that landed me in trouble was also a coping strategy. One I didn't realise that I needed at the time, but that saved me nonetheless from a reality too daunting for my young self to understand.

You see, growing up autistic and undiagnosed brought its challenges.

CHALLENGES OF GROWING UP AUTISTIC

- » Experiencing a lot of anxiety.
- » Finding change difficult.
- » Despising group work.
- » Being called 'bossy'.
- » Struggling to interpret and follow instructions.
- » Being unable to cope with not finishing something.
- » Struggling to switch focus between tasks.
- » Experiencing sensory difficulties.

» Frequently interrupting people.*
» Finding people don't understand your intense interests (like BOOKS).
» Being unable to fall asleep.
» Misunderstanding social situations.
» Struggling to use common sense.
» Copying characters on TV.
» Feeling like a misfit.

Burying myself in books and fantasy lands protected me from these things. My brain created a safety blanket for myself that I could delve under whenever things began to get too much. And that worked, for quite a long while.

There are a lot of things that would have made my life a lot easier, though, and that I wish little me had known.

Dear little Emily,

Here are some things that I would like you to know, with the hope that they will make your life a bit easier.

When your teacher tells you to 'wait outside', they don't actually mean outside the building. They mean in the corridor, by the classroom door.

The children in your class really do not want to be given your small paper fish at going home time. This is in no way a reflection on you or your creativity, but on their lack of imagination and admiration for originality.

---

* For me, it is likely that this, along with my excessive talkativeness, could be better explained by my Attention Deficit Hyperactivity Disorder (ADHD) – another fairly misunderstood neurodevelopmental condition that a high proportion of autistic people also have.[14] But when you're both autistic and have ADHD, it's hard to know where one starts and the other ends. I just know now that my brain is different – and that's okay.

When those kids tell you that a game is their game, they don't mean that. They are being mean. You don't have to ask permission to play that game. You can play it wherever and whenever you like, if it brings you joy.

Some questions are not meant to be answered, even though they have been asked. If you answer them, you are 'talking back' and that is rude. Even though they asked it, you are in the wrong. And yes, it is impossible to tell which questions are meant to be answered and which ones are not.

When an adult tells you to not disturb them, this does not mean that you shouldn't disturb them if something serious is happening. If there is a fire, please tell them.

When someone asks you what you did on the weekend, they don't want to know exactly what you did from the minute you woke up until you went to bed. A highlight or two will suffice.

People contradict themselves all of the time. Especially adults. They will tell you not to do something and then they will do it themselves. Don't question this or you will get in trouble. Even though it doesn't make sense.

When people say that the world is going to end, they do not mean that the world is actually going to end.

People exaggerate things a lot. When a kid in your class says he climbed ten mountains over the weekend, he probably didn't.

Hold on to your imagination for as long as you possibly can. It will protect you.

People will tell you that you are weird. It's okay to be hurt by that but just know that it is because you are incredibly special.

Love, Emily

CHAPTER TWO

'why else are we here if not to live with
unreasonable passion for things'
—butterflies rising

Peering through the glass, which is stained with droplets and greasy fingerprints, I fix my eyes on the water, fascinated. It is not blue, like I have always imagined the sea to be, but a murky grey, a reflection of the dark clouds circling above. Waves hungrily gnaw the side of the vessel, gurgling with each bite. It is not enticing. In fact, there are very few people standing on the deck, most preferring to gather inside in the warmth, away from the strong wind. Still, I stand here, transfixed by the waves, wondering if there are dolphins dancing jubilantly around us.

I know that there are dolphins in the English Channel. Bottlenose dolphins, specifically. One of the most common and widely recognised dolphin species. I admire the resilience they must have to live around here. I should think their friends in more tropical climates are much happier.

'Seen any?' Dad appears at my side, tall enough to see straight over the glass.

'No. Can you lift me up?' I ask, imagining the crystal-clear view he must have.

'Not out here.' He chuckles. 'It's too windy. We should go and join Mummy inside.'

I shake my head. I am not ready. 'Not yet.'

I'd started my research on dolphins at the end of the last school term, beginning to write a non-fiction book about them during breaktime while the rest of the girls played netball. They had asked me to join in, because I am goalkeeper, but it wasn't a practice day. One of the girls, Ruth, had looked at me as if she were looking at something unpleasant. Like how I scrunch my nose up when I eat a berry too sweet or too bitter. I hadn't been sure what she had meant by that look, but my thoughts soon returned to dolphins. I'd wished briefly that the girls were interested, so I would have some companionship at breaktime, but the excitement of designing my book soon took over. I'd fixated on it for hours. My brain can do that very easily.

My book is finished, but I still think about dolphins a lot. They are highly intelligent, friendly and social animals. They are very chatty (like me!) and are good at communicating, making sounds like whistles, squeaks, yelps and groans. They can even recognise themselves in mirrors, at a younger age than humans can. They are wonderful animals. It makes me happy that their friends get excited with them, instead of leaving them alone.

I am distracted from my thoughts by a sudden movement of water in the distance. A splash of green on the horizon.

'Reckon that could have been one?' Dad asks, zipping up his jacket as a strong gust of wind blows right through us. I grab onto the barrier, steadying myself. My stomach lurches like a wave is rushing through it as I catch sight of the feisty water below the deck. I wonder what it would be like to fall. How the biting cold would feel against my skin. I wonder if I would be able to swim. Sometimes, when I am upset by the girls at school, I wish I could be swallowed up.

I feel a gentle nudge on my shoulder.

'Well? Could it have been?' Dad repeats his question.

'Possibly.' I nod, solemnly. 'They are probably scared by the ferry. It can't be good for them.'

I know I won't see a dolphin, but the look of water is enchanting – the reflections of the ripples in the light captivate me. My eyes follow the lines they create, noticing the shapes formed by the foam.

'Did you know that they use echolocation to find their food and explore their surroundings? They make click noises, like this,' I explain, imitating the *click, click* I imagine them to make. 'Then those noises bounce off of the objects to show them how far away they are!'

Dad grins. 'Did you know that's physics!'

I groan and pretend to push him playfully. 'I hate science!'

I really do hate science. I don't like having to work in groups and look at circuits and make smelly potions. They are just batteries and wires and liquids. Dad loves science and is always trying to convince me that it is great. But I would rather read about something interesting. Like dolphins.

'C'mon. We need to go in now.'

I stare wistfully out at the water, hoping for my eyes to catch sight of something. Unfortunately, I have no such luck. With a sigh, I turn around and follow Dad across the deck, back through the heavy doors into the ferry.

In 1925, 18 years prior to Kanner's so-called 'discovery' of autism, Grunya Sukhareva published a paper.[1] She was a child psychiatrist working at a clinic in Moscow, where she had identified six boys who appeared to show what she called 'schizoid psychopathy', which she later changed to 'autistic psychopathy'.[2] These boys shared similar characteristics to both Leo Kanner and Hans Asperger's samples (we will talk a little bit about Asperger later).

As Steve Silberman explains in his bestselling autism history *NeuroTribes*,[3] one of the boys Sukhareva saw was an extremely gifted violinist who gained a place at the Moscow Conservatory. Another knew everything about the war of 1812 before he was ten. Another's knowledge of politics in the emerging Soviet Union was fascinating. Sukhareva described this commonality as 'strong interests pursued exclusively'.[4]

What Sukhareva was recognising were these boys' *special interests*. This term is now widely used to describe the specific and intense interests and passions that autistic people can have. Not everyone likes this description, particularly because the word 'special' can be used in a derogatory way towards disabled people. Some prefer 'specific interests' or 'intense interests', but language is constantly evolving. Irrespective of the term, these interests are very important to autistic people – and Sukhareva identified their relevance years earlier than Kanner or Asperger did. Unfortunately, her contribution to the development of our understanding of autism was overlooked for some time and Kanner received the credit. Sukhareva's paper was published in Russian and translated into German the following year, but not into English until 1996 when British child psychiatrist Sula Wolff came across it.[5] It was only later, when the work of Dr Judith Gould and Dr Lorna Wing shed a light on Asperger's 1944 paper,[6] 'Autistic Psychopathy in Childhood,'[7] and Steve Silberman uncovered the link between Kanner and Asperger (mainly a man named Georg Frankl),[8] that other influences in autism history were recognised.

It is now known that Grunya Sukhareva's work was pioneering; and it is argued that her description is very similar to the diagnostic criteria listed in the American Psychiatric Association's *Diagnostic and Statistical Manual of Mental*

Disorders (DSM-5) today.[9] In this key publication, the diagnostic criterion for autism (which is <u>not</u> a mental disorder!) include 'restricted, repetitive patterns of behaviour, interests or activities'[10] as one of the core features. Special interests form a big part of this.

I am unsure why this language around 'restrictive and repetitive interests' needs to be quite so negative. Some researchers do conclude that special interests impact autistic people's functioning negatively[11] – and, yes, I suppose it is hard to wash the dishes when my brain is intensely fixated on something else. In all seriousness, there are times when special interests *can* be problematic and time-consuming. They can take over, becoming all-encompassing. Sometimes this is okay, but sometimes this can affect a person's wellbeing.

However, there is also evidence showing the positive impact that special interests have on us and their association with good wellbeing.[12] A study of nearly two thousand young autistic people highlighted the joy that their special interests brought them, suggesting that they rarely interfere with functioning and can lead to strong careers and benefits not only for individuals but also for society[13] (not that we should have to benefit society to be valued).

Special interests, I think, are essential for an autistic person's navigation of life. They can provide a structure, a certainty, around which the individual can build their life. They can provide an escape, where enjoyment and relaxation can be sought when the demands and stress of daily life are too much. When the person is able to base their job or socialisation around this interest, it can help them to make friends, to have positive interactions with others and to have a fulfilling career – because, contrary to popular belief, a lot of autistic people do want these things.

Dolphins were, as far as I can remember, the first special

interest I had. It didn't last very long. My brain likes to chop and change its focus as quickly as the weather. I become heavily invested in a topic for a period of a few days, sometimes longer, then get bored and move on to something else. This is rather typical of autistic ADHDers especially. I have had some special interests which have lasted longer. Especially books, which were very consistent throughout my childhood.

SPECIAL OR 'SPECIFIC' INTERESTS I HAVE HAD THROUGHOUT MY LIFE

- » Books
- » Dolphins
- » Harry Potter
- » Writing
- » More books
- » The *Friends* TV show
- » Musicals
- » Autism*

Special interests can be really cool, and I would love to see autistic people's interests nurtured from childhood for the much-needed safe haven they provide.

Back through the doors, the echoey sound bouncing off the steel walls hits me at once. Shrill voices sound from all directions. Young children squeal in excitement as they are

---

* Autistic culture is finding out you are autistic and all of a sudden your special interest *is* autism and you want to know EVERYTHING you possibly can about it and talk about it non-stop . . . Hence the existence of this book.

wheeled along the marble flooring on their small ride-on suitcases.

I follow Dad along the aisle, bordered by rows of seats and tables. I hear the tills before I see the shops. They open and close, a series of earsplitting crashes. Coins clink together, a hand rummaging through them for change. Somewhere in the crowd, a mum tries desperately to screw a lid onto a baby's bottle, him screaming in her arms. I press my nails against the palm of my hand, focusing on the sting.

We join Mum, Thomas and Jessica, the three of them sat at a table in the food court. Thomas and Jessica gulp down a jam sandwich each, crumbs glued to their sticky fingers. Thomas's legs are swinging back and forth restlessly. I perch by the aisle next to him, cautious to not touch the stains left by the previous occupants, and feel my leg begin to bob up and down like a buoy in the ocean. This movement keeps me afloat in a sea of noise, the inevitability of the repetition somehow comforting.

'Jam sandwich?' Mum offers. Dad takes his gratefully. I shake my head, my stomach churning. I wish I was still looking for dolphins. There is a family gathered by the closest window, two young children lacing the glass with greasy fingers. From here, the water looks murky and unappealing.

Thomas finishes his sandwich, wiping his hands over his shirt before Mum can get to them with a wipe. A cheeky smile spreads across his lips. He sticks his tongue out at me.

'La, la, la, la, la, la, laa . . .' he repeats, shaking his head from side to side.

I stare at the floor, trying to ignore the irritation welling up inside of me. Mum and Dad tell me not to react, because when I do, apparently it makes the situation worse.

Behind us, there is a clatter of metal as the cutlery tray is filled to the brim. The kitchen door swings open, plates scratching and clanging against each other. The smell of salty bacon and fried onions fills the air and I pinch my nose to stop myself gagging. I don't like it when the world becomes loud like this and I can't drag my thoughts away to something comforting. Outside was calmer. Quieter. I could think. The air was fresh and the smell neutral. There were no lights burning my eyes. No brother making annoying noises. My leg bounces higher with each beat, until my knee hits the table and I flinch in pain.

'Stop it!' I snarl, hitting my fist on the table. Dad shoots Thomas a look, then one at me. I have learned that this means I should be quiet.

My fists scrunch up at my side, my body tensing. A large group of people suddenly appear, having turned the corner in search of the entrance to the deck. A dozen of them bustle past the table, one knocking my arm with their rucksack. I glare at them, my chest tightening and then releasing as they fade into the distance. Then Thomas pulls at my sleeve.

'Stop it!' I shout, tears of frustration pricking my eyelids. I don't want to be here. I want to be on my own.

'Be quiet,' Mum hisses angrily, tired from the ten hours we have journeyed so far. 'You can't have a go at him when you were doing it earlier too.'

Anger swirls in my stomach. I wasn't doing *this*; I was singing a song lyric. Because I liked the way the words sounded in my mouth. I wasn't doing it purposefully to upset anyone. 'I was singing! And he's only doing it to upset me!'

'Then don't be so sensitive,' Dad says.

I throw my chair backwards as I stand up and storm towards the toilets. I race past the sink and force my way into a cubicle, slamming the door shut as I collapse onto the toilet seat. The sudden change in volume is glaringly obvious, almost startling. The noise is fainter, dulled, muffled. As if a sponge has been placed over a speaker. I am now acutely aware of the rise and fall of my breaths, uneven as fury bubbles in my chest. They are not being fair. It is not the first time I have been told not to be so sensitive. That I need to learn to deal with the things that irritate me. When I tell them it's not fair, Dad tells me that life is not fair. Am I too fussy? Too spoiled? Why can't I just stay calm?

As I readjust my shorts, I notice they still have a label in them. Unusual, because checking there are no labels lingering in my clothes is a staple of my morning routine. This one, like most of my clothes, says 'Marks & Spencer'. I'm not meant to get my clothes from there anymore, I am told at school. But that is where Mum shops. I rub my lower back where the label has been rubbing and realise it has been irritating me all day. I tug at it, ripping away the fabric from the seam. Bits of thread loosen as it falls off in my hands. Yet, even though it's now gone, I sense the prick of it against my skin – a feeling it has taken me all day to process.

After my breathing becomes less frantic, I exit the cubicle and splash water onto my face at the sink. I just want to get home, where I can climb under my bedsheets and shut my eyes. Where I am alone, and away from everyone else. Where it is silent, and I can think about dolphins.

As an autistic child, with no understanding of my neurotype or of sensory difficulties, I had no idea that what I was experiencing was not something everyone experienced. People around me did not know this either, because I did not have seemingly obvious meltdowns when things were noisy. I would snap, I would storm off, I would argue and I would cry, but the chaos in my head was invisible. All that was seen was a child who was argumentative, impatient, or had a 'short fuse'. The fact I had reached a point of being unable to continue regulating myself, or of being so overloaded sensory-wise that I could not think, was hidden, the triggers passing by unnoticed.

My earliest memories of sensory discomfort concern the feeling of mud on my hands and sand between my toes. Even worse, sand stuck to my skin after playing in the sea. I could sit and pick the grains off one by one, but one grain would still escape and my irritability from it would inevitably result in me arguing with someone. Then there were coats, which I often point-blank refused to wear, even in the freezing cold. Too restrictive. And of course, my brother's sniffing and irritating noises, made usually with the sole purpose of agitating me. No wonder the sentence 'I hate my brother' features on several pages in my childhood diaries.

Sensory difficulties are very common among autistic people and increase our stress and anxiety.[14] They can make day-to-day life difficult to tolerate, whether they relate to noise, tastes, smells, lights or textures of materials, like clothing. For instance, *who* decided that tights should be a thing?

ITEMS OF CLOTHING THAT SHOULD NOT EXIST (BECAUSE ... SENSORY ISSUES)

» Tights
» Skinny jeans
» Socks
» Ties
» Tights
» Anything with labels
» Scarves
» Turtleneck tops or jumpers
» TIGHTS
» Anything with sequins

Learning about my sensory needs later in my life was a massive revelation for me. Did you know that some people can focus on the task they are doing, even when there are irritating background noises? Sometimes people don't notice these noises until someone like me points them out. Some aren't even affected by five minutes of processing more sensory information than usual, let alone left exhausted with depleted energy supplies. Some don't find conversations in busy rooms any more difficult than conversations in quiet rooms. And not everyone gets headaches from bright lights. This might sound like basic information to you, but this was mind-boggling to me, because I didn't realise that my brain processed things any differently. But it does. Research studies have found that autistic people have an increased auditory perceptual capacity,[15] meaning that our brains process more sensory information at any one time than non-autistic people's brains. This can lead to heightened levels of sensory sensitivities.[16]

We try to learn to manage our sensory needs, but sometimes sensory overload is unavoidable. Sometimes our brains just can't handle all the different sensory input, and we shut down. Or we freeze. Or we meltdown.

Let me explain what sensory overload is like.

Imagine that my brain is a kettle. The water filling up the kettle is sensory information. The kettle being switched on and bringing the water to the boil is my brain processing this information. But, what happens when there is too much sensory information for the kettle to handle? It starts to bubble and overboil, and it could explode.

Like the water bubbling in the kettle as it heats up, the sensory information in my brain begins to get muddled up. It sends more intense but more jumbled-up instructions to different parts of my brain and body, catapulting me into overload. My brain begins to spasm because it can't work out what information it needs and what information it can filter out. As it all gathers in spiderwebs, it begins to hurt my sensory organs like my ears, and the water in the kettle bubbles and boils until it nearly bursts.

This is sensory overload. When the loud noises, the bright lights, the strong smells, the peculiar tastes and the uncomfortable sensations you can feel all merge together and feel unbearable. There is too much water in the kettle. Too much information to process. My brain, like the kettle, is overwhelmed, and has to do something to fix the situation. So, it shuts down, melts down or panics, or it grows irritable, frustrated or moody – all the result of overstimulation.

THINGS THAT CAN HELP WITH SENSORY STUFF

- » Noise-cancelling headphones
- » Earplugs
- » Ear defenders
- » Tinted glasses
- » Sensory friendly clothing, such as clothes without seams
- » Weighted blankets
- » Chew toys
- » Dim lighting
- » Sensory toys
- » Compression clothing
- » Sensory swings
- » Stimming

Stimming is repetitive behaviour that helps an individual to regulate themselves. It can serve to reduce stress or anxiety, to seek or reduce sensory input (for example by the individual focusing on a specific feeling rather than the overwhelm around them), or to express enjoyment and release joy. It can include hand-flapping, rocking, spinning or jumping, but also other less recognisable behaviours, such as twirling hair or flicking a rubber repeatedly. Me bouncing my leg up and down could class as stimming. I often do this at times of heightened sensory input.

Hypersensitivity to the sensory environment can be difficult to manage, and has impacted my quality of life at times, but I also think that occasionally it can be special to experience the world at such an intensity. The beauty of music, the softness of fabrics, the taste of air, the smell of familiar places can be so vibrant. Literature almost wholly focuses on the negatives – and I do understand why, because sensory difficulties can be debilitating. But let's spend a moment appreciating some of our strengths.

Enhanced pitch perception among autistic people has been demonstrated in literature for years. Rimland and Fein in 1988 found that 5 per cent of autistic people showed perfect (or absolute) pitch judgement compared to 0.05 per cent of the general population.[17] An increased ability to discriminate pitches and an increased long-term memory of melodies was found among autistic children with no musical training in 2014.[18] That's pretty cool, right? Furthermore, attention to detail of sound and being able to be absorbed by musical projects can also provide joy for some autistic people[19] – though this was definitely not true for me. I did *not* enjoy playing the flute.

Sensory needs are not always obvious, but even if they don't cause visible meltdowns, they can often trigger emotions such as irritability, restlessness or anxiety. It is so important to try to identify these needs and the triggers for different behaviours. I understand why mine weren't recognised when

I was younger: because I internalised or 'masked' much of it, and it wasn't until I was older when my responses weren't appropriate for my age that it became much more obvious. But even then, nobody considered *why* I could be experiencing such things. I would always consider, when looking at a child presenting with sensory difficulties, whether they could be autistic. Because not knowing is hard.

Especially when you are desperately trying to fit in.

CHAPTER THREE

'As the river runs wild through the canyons, so does peace run wild through the soul. For no matter what stands tall around you, deep within, you are free, you are whole.'
—Morgan Harper Nichols

The belief that I was weird was not so much a conclusion I came to as it was a fact I just grew up knowing. To me, it was as obvious as it was that the sky is blue. I knew for certain that I was different; and other children showed me that that wasn't a good thing.

I can't pinpoint exactly when I realised that I was different, but it was at some stage in my early primary-school years. It became obvious to me pretty quickly that a lot of the things I cared about, other children didn't, and that a lot of the things they cared about, I didn't.

THINGS OTHER KIDS CARED ABOUT

- » Football, specifically Chelsea FC
- » Pop music
- » *The Twilight Saga*
- » Make-up
- » Boybands
- » *The X Factor*
- » 'Hanging out' at the park

THINGS I CARED ABOUT

- » Books
- » My homework*
- » More books
- » Going to the library
- » Harry Potter
- » Even more books

The fact that I was different stood out to me every day. Adults repeatedly said that I talked too much, too loudly and too quickly (*cough cough*, ADHD). Teachers said that I didn't pay attention to instructions, even though I tried my hardest to and just didn't understand them. Other children laughed at me for not understanding jokes or sarcasm, even though nobody seemed to laugh at them when they didn't understand the big words that I used – which I didn't think were even that big!

You see, I loved words. I was always reading; and if I wasn't reading, I was writing. Diary after diary, story after story.

I wrote my first diary when I was five and visited New Zealand for the second time. A country of beauty, where my father is from. In his late twenties, he decided to leave for the first time to go travelling. His first stop was England. That is how, one September afternoon, he found himself in The Cat and Fiddle, a quaint little pub in Hertfordshire, watching my mother and her friends amble in as this was their local. His eyes fell on her. Seven months later, he got down on one knee on one of the 300 bridges in Venice. A Venetian gondolier

---

* I may have been the only child ever to have got excited when our teachers gave us homework. Yet I still wondered why I was at the bottom of the popularity chain.

passed on the water underneath, the music of a *barcarole* filling the air. In my mum's excitement to run to the other side of the bridge to see the gondola pass, she missed this. So, Dad tried again – and sure enough, they found themselves engaged. He never went back home except to visit.

I don't remember my first time visiting his homeland; I was only two years old. My second trip, though, is well detailed in a pink notebook I was gifted by my grandmother. Or as well detailed as is possible for a five-year-old, regardless of her already blossoming love for writing. This diary begins with a very comprehensive packing list, including 'family' (I don't know how I thought I was going to get to the 'aueroport' without them), 'parstport' (five-year-old me was definitely not responsible for remembering to pack this), 'dovay' (had no one told me I wasn't allowed to bring my duvet on a plane?) and 'all cloths' (I wonder how much difficulty my parents had dragging the entirety of the contents of my wardrobe to the other side of the world). The list does also state 'trosis', 'scort', 'shorts' and 'tits', but I'm not sure whose tits this five-year-old was packing!

The rest of the diary is filled with lines after lines of my big blue-inked scrawls. By the time I started school, I was already writing pages after pages. I don't remember learning to write, only learning to rein this desire in. Although my school reports from this age describe my writing as 'beautiful', they also encourage me to remember what I was meant to be writing, as I had a 'habit of turning most writing into a story'. Producing reams of work was only partly because I loved to write though, and partly because when I was told to 'write as much as you can', I didn't realise this instruction wasn't literal. So, I would hand in twenty double sides of A4 instead of two sides like everyone else.

My literality carved its way into lots of parts of my life.

I was incredibly obedient, not realising there were often caveats to instructions. Other children weren't particularly fond of my keenness in the classroom. Or the praise I received for being the smartest in the class. And I didn't know that teachers didn't find me correcting their spelling and grammar on every single PowerPoint slide and handout helpful. I hadn't yet understood that their 'thank yous' had an edge of irritation. I took everyone and everything at face value. Sadly, that made me stand out.

It seemed that whoever I turned to, I was different. And I knew that meant I was weird, long before other children told me this too – although when they did, it hurt even more.

On the first day of term after France, I walk down the path onto the school grounds, clutching my satchel tightly. It isn't the one I usually take to school – that one is covered in sand from holiday because I had insisted on taking it to the beach. Mum has given me my old one instead. It's pink, with a *Hannah Montana* print on it. It used to be my favourite bag, until the girls told me that it was 'babyish'. Last year they all had these bags; and when I got one for my birthday, I was so excited to be like everyone else. I wore it proudly on the first day in September, only to find that they had ditched theirs in favour of black handbags and that these ones were suddenly uncool. I can never keep up with them.

I begin to feel tears threatening my eyes as the school building appears on my right. I don't know if it is because of the bright morning sun blinding me or the thought of the day ahead. The butterflies in my stomach tell me that it is the latter. Despite being overly talkative, I don't know who I will chat to, I don't know who I will eat lunch with and I don't know who will pair up with me in PE.

Then I see them, the cause of the butterflies. Four of them standing together on the playground, gathered around a Match Attax folder like a swarm of bees. These football trading cards are the new in-thing. It takes only seconds for the blonde girl to look up from the card she is holding and clock me. Ruth. The queen bee, as my books would say.

She marches straight over, the other three girls at her heel. Puffs of dust from the playground shoot into the air with their every step. My body tenses in anticipation, as if preparing for a blow.

'Hi Emily. How was your holiday?' she asks. Her face is all scrunched up, like someone has pinched her nose and refused to let go. Perhaps if she smiled, she would be pretty. But a pout plasters the spot where a smile should be.

'It was okay,' I reply, suspiciously. Uncomfortable, I sling my bag onto the other shoulder. She stares at it for a moment, evidently unimpressed, before moving her stare to my hair. It is brushed into a ponytail, my fringe flopping over the bridge of my eyebrow and tucking behind my ear.

'Did you even brush your hair this morning? It doesn't look like you did.'

'I did.' I run my fingers through it anxiously.

'It doesn't look like it, does it?' She turns to the other three, dramatically. One of them is my friend, but when she is with *her*, she is different. She nods in agreement, but she doesn't look at me. Instead, she stares sheepishly at the ground, shuffling her feet uneasily.

'It looks like a bird's nest,' Ruth says, before turning and walking away again. The others follow her once again, like clingy puppies pining for affection.

I don't always understand unspoken cues, but I know I am not welcome to follow them.

I feel a wave of sickness rush through me. I don't understand why my hair looks bad. Mum brushed it for me this morning and she always does it nicely. I like it when she does it.

I wait for the school bell to go, a noise that hurts my ears every time. When it finally sounds, I rush into the classroom and pull out the book that I am reading – *A Diary of a Young Girl* by Anne Frank. I have already read it twice before, once in Year 2, then again in Year 4. Each time that I read it, I understand things that I hadn't the previous time. It gives me a deeper understanding of Anne and Nazi Germany.

The other children pile into the classroom after me. I bury my head in the pages, savouring the smell – wood mixed with a touch of vanilla – to desperately try to ignore their chatter.

Ruth marches in. Sashaying past my desk, she says loudly, 'Abigail's party was fun, wasn't it?'

I glance up. I didn't know that Abigail had had a party. I thought she would have invited me. Ruth sits down at the table opposite. As her eyes meet mine, her lips turn slightly upwards. I study her face for a moment, trying to read her expression, but quickly give up. I shift my gaze back to the words on the page, now blurry.

The morning passes slowly. I don't focus properly; my thoughts are with the half-finished chapter of my book. I don't like leaving things half-finished. Breaktime comes, and I trek out onto the playground with everyone else. The girls in our class form a circle. I sit in it with them, wistfully thinking about my book laying on my desk in the classroom. I would rather be reading, but I don't want to be left out.

Turns out, I don't have the choice.

'Emily, we're going to have a private talk,' Ruth announces. She twiddles her hair with her thumb, remains of pink polish scuffing the edges of the nail.

I look at her uncertainly. 'What do you mean?'

'You need to leave because we're going to have a private talk.'

I look around the group of 15 girls. A few of them are grinning at her. Most of them are staring at the ground, picking at their clothes, or fiddling with their shoelaces.

'All . . . all of you?' I stammer.

Ruth sighs dramatically and makes a gesture with her hand, shooing me away.

'But . . . why?'

'You're so weird,' she says, not even looking at me this time.

I stand up, my legs shaking beneath me like jelly. My mouth moves, as if to form words, but none come out. I stare at them for a second longer, then turn towards the rest of the playground. My eyes scan for anyone I know, anyone I can walk to, but there isn't anybody.

I walk away, shoulders slumped. Her words circle around my head. She is right, I *am* weird.

Somehow, my peers seemed to know as young as the age of seven or eight that I was different to them. Kids should be the ones in charge of autism assessments – or at least deciding who should be referred for one – because they sniff us out a mile away and they don't hesitate in letting us know that we are different.

It is sadly very common for autistic children to be bullied and left out by their peers.[1] We stand out, for whatever reason. I don't know why children seem to pick on those who appear different to them, but they do.

In one survey, 75 per cent of autistic young people reported having been bullied.[2] But I think the figure is higher. I think most autistic people have found themselves a victim of bullying at some point in their lives, because we don't always conform to the majority, we don't always understand social cues and people like to make a joke out of us. Because they think it's funny, or it makes some twisted part of themselves feel good. But none of that is a reflection on us, just on them.

It took me a long time to come to the conclusion that I had been subject to bullying. I was never hit, kicked or punched. Ruth's verbal insults weren't explicitly awful. But I felt intimidated and isolated, day after day, made to feel bad about myself for years to come. And that is bullying.

THINGS THAT YOU SHOULD KNOW IF YOU HAVE BEEN BULLIED

» It wasn't your fault.
» You don't deserve what happened to you.
» If you didn't tell anyone, that doesn't mean it was any less real.
» It's okay to tell someone now, even if it's years later.
» It's okay if what was said and done to you still affects you now.
» It's okay if you still feel hurt and angry.
» Bullying is recognised as a cause of trauma.
» You are not a bad person.
» You are loved.

The worst part of it all was that I believed them. I believed that I was weird, and I believed that I needed to do something about it.

By the age of eight, I had already become fairly accustomed to copying others in order to fit in; but from what I can remember, up until this point, this was mostly an unconscious process. I knew when I walked into a situation that I hadn't been in before, when I didn't have the social template in my head of what to say or do, that I would turn to those around me and follow them. For a lot of it seemed innate to them. I can look back now and recognise this, but at the time I wasn't actively thinking of what I was doing and why.

That is, until the bullying caused me to make a conscious choice to hide myself and try to fit in.

I can feel their eyes on my back without even seeing them. They bore into my skin, freezing my blood. Their sniggers and their whispers send jolts through me. Like rushes of electricity.

I can't concentrate on my work, even though we are learning about the Tudors, which I usually love. I am fascinated by their clothing and how they wore so many uncomfortable layers yet managed to get on with their life. I would find it incredibly itchy and difficult to do anything at all in their clothes. Mum and Dad are taking me to Hampton Court Palace soon. I love learning. I throw myself into it, desperate to learn everything I can. Unless we are asked to work in groups, then my interest dwindles. The other kids don't care about the work and mess around. I try to get it done and then am told that I am bossy. When I have learned to sit quietly, then the task doesn't get finished and the teacher tells us off. I can't win no matter what I do. Working on my own is a much better option.

The task we have been given today has yet to captivate me. Every time I feel myself becoming entranced by it, a whisper knocks my focus. It is Ruth as usual. This morning she told me that the top I wore to youth group last night was babyish. *Everything* about me seems to be babyish to her. But I like my top. It has a little robin on it. And it is blue, my favourite colour. My grandpa says it is lovely. Now, though, I plan to stuff it at the back of my cupboard so Mum can't find it again.

Instead of looking at my work, my gaze falls on two of my

classmates having a conversation in front of me. Without really realising, I find myself engrossed by them. I am not interested in the content of what they are saying, but in their movements. I watch the way they take it in turns to talk and respond to each other, the way their hands move succinctly as if props aiding their communication and the way their faces change as they take in what the other is saying. I wonder whether they are controlling their expressions or if they are subconscious. I wonder whether my face looks like theirs when I talk.

I watch the two of them move their eyebrows and alter the wideness of their eyes and mouth as they speak. I copy them. When their eyebrows lift a little, I lift mine. When their eyes widen, I widen mine. When their lips tilt slightly upwards, I tilt mine upwards too. The trouble is, I feel like a puppet with a smile painted on.

I know that my face is weird. Ruth has told me so. So now I've taken an interest in how other people guide their faces and have resolved to practising my expressions. I don't think my face always matches how I am feeling. This morning I practised my happy face in front of the bathroom mirror. Except the longer I stared at my face, the more alien it looked and the less the expression made sense. Nevertheless, I must continue to try. It is tiring trying to be aware of my facial expression all the time, but I don't have a choice. I want the other children to like me.

I didn't know it then, but what I was doing was developing the art of masking. Something many autistic people are very skilled in.

Autistic masking is where autistic people essentially pretend to be neurotypical. It is a process of us learning how neurotypical people behave and react to things, and learning to mimic this for ourselves so that we don't stand out. Not all autistic people mask. But I am one of those who grew up doing so and continue to in many parts of my life.

And it is exhausting.

EXAMPLES OF AUTISTIC MASKING

» Making eye contact even when it's uncomfortable to avoid being told you are rude.
» Learning a sort of script to know what to say in different social situations.
» Practising facial expressions in the mirror and actively controlling your expressions.
» Controlling the tone of your voice to make sure you sound interested.
» Suppressing stims.*
» Suppressing the urge to talk non-stop about your special interests.
» Copying the reactions of TV characters in similar situations.†
» Wearing clothes that are itchy or painful because you think you have to.
» Holding in authentic reactions until you get home, when it then comes out in a meltdown or shutdown.
» Pretending that noise doesn't hurt your ears.

---

* See explanation in Chapter Two, page 34.
† This really does not always go well. Especially when Tracy Beaker is your character of choice (I'm talking to younger me . . .). Copying her reactions was not well received. Anne of Green Gables wasn't much better either. Speaking poetically in verse had various reactions from my friends, though I believed it sounded elegant.

» Mirroring other people's actions in unfamiliar situations.
» Suppressing instinctive autistic behaviours like autistic joy* because it's 'too much' for other people.

There is a massive misconception that if we are copying those around us, then we're being 'fake' and 'lying'. And I too often ask myself who I am. What is *actually* me, when so much of me is a collection of personality traits and social skills I have picked up from other people? But I now know that there is a need for us to mask; that is why many of us who are able to have grown up doing so. It is a defence mechanism, a survival strategy, or an (often but not always) unconscious way of our brain looking out for us.

And for some autistic people, masking occurs due to a physical presence of risk. One such risk is a type of therapy some autistic people are forced into from a young age. This is called Applied Behavioural Analysis, or ABA. Its proponents say that it is lifesaving, essential therapy for autistic children to ensure they have a chance of some kind of quality of life, but it actually serves to teach autistic kids to pretend to be neurotypical. They are rewarded for 'good' (i.e., neurotypical) behaviour – for example, making eye contact and socialising in a neurotypical way – and punished for 'bad' (i.e., autistic) behaviour, like stimming. In some forms of ABA, autistic children are deprived of having their basic needs met to 'teach' them to ask for them to be met 'properly'. Even when punishments aren't used and needs aren't explicitly denied, children are still taught to suppress their autistic traits. ABA does not ask why the child is distressed in certain situations but forces them instead to tolerate them and then rewards them for doing so. It does not look at making things work

---

*   More about this later.

for their brain but tries to coerce them to conform. It believes that children can be desensitised to loud noises and clothes that make their bodies sore and believes they can be rewarded into not stimming and making eye contact.

ABA teaches autistic people to mask heavily, which increases their risk of suicide,[3] and has been shown to increase PTSD symptoms.[4] Presumably most ABA practitioners are unaware of these negative consequences, refuse to listen to what autistic people tell them or aren't fussed by the evidence suggesting it is ineffective[5] because they have seen it 'work' for themselves. Yet its efficacy is not supported by evidence. A 2018 Cochrane Review, a gold-standard systematic review of health research, explored whether early behavioural intervention such as ABA (or Positive Behaviour Support, as is now commonly used, also with limited success)[6] improves autistic people's lives.[7] The findings do not suggest it did. There was merely weak evidence of small improvements after two years, which could also have been achieved by autistic children not receiving the interventions. One 2022 paper showed no difference in improvement between autistic children who received behavioural therapy and those who didn't.[8] Meanwhile, it is causing trauma.[9] While teaching autistic people that their needs do not matter and forcing them to mask. This can have serious effects on autistic people's mental health as they grow older.[10]

A lot of autistic people grow up masking because it is not safe for us to be our authentic autistic selves. This is especially true for Black autistic people, for whom not masking can carry an even greater risk. Behaviour in Black children is frequently interpreted differently to the same behaviour in white children,[11] and the response to them can be more aggressive.[12] Black people are more likely to experience harm for authentic autistic behaviour than white autistic people are, particularly at the hands of the police.[13] In 2017, in one instance of many, Richard Hayes, an unarmed Black autistic 18-year-old, was shot by a Chicago police officer, Khalil Muhammad. Richard had simply been running along the street, having been reported missing by his carer.[14] These dangers are not limited to the US.[15] In April 2022, a 17-year-old Black nonspeaking autistic boy was locked up at Gatwick Airport facing deportation to Nigeria. His family had reported him missing. The boy was not Nigerian, but because he couldn't speak and had no identification on him, he was taken to be detained at an immigration centre.[16] These are very real risks for Black autistic people, increasing the need they may feel to mask to survive.[17]

It is clear that the risks for some autistic people are more significant than for others, particularly for Black autistic people and those who are unable to mask. White privilege and my lower support needs mean that I have never been at risk of physical harm for unmasking, and I will never experience the horrors that some autistic people face.

Although masking would become detrimental to my mental health, it has also been helpful at times to be able to pass as neurotypical. It made me feel more protected and reduced the number of comments I got suggesting that I was weird. I don't seem to be as good at masking as I used to be, though. I'm not sure if that is because adulting requires a form of masking I haven't yet mastered, or if it is because my brain is so tired from the past 22 years.

CHAPTER FOUR

'I like school and I hate it,
that world within a world of arbitrary rules.'
—Jonny Heath

I am now 11 years old, and I am standing at the gate to my new secondary school. It is the first day and the excitement I feel is somewhat surprising for someone who despises change. But, getting away from Ruth and the other girls feels like a fresh start. I am looking forward to playing pranks on French teachers, mixing potions in chemistry and cooking brownies in food tech like they do in Enid Blyton's *Malory Towers* and *St Clare's*. Only, this school is even better because there is no swimming pool.

Confident in the knowledge that I won't have to go swimming (my sole criteria on deciding what secondary school I would go to), I take a step forward onto the school grounds. My light-brown hair is swept into a ponytail and my sweaty hands grip onto the straps of my backpack. This one is blue, from a market stall in the local town, because the rules dictate that our bags must be blue. I am pleased to know what is expected of me but I'm not sure why bags have to be a particular colour. I notice that the thread of mine is already beginning to fray at the seams.

The school building looms ahead, a gravel path littered with dozens of students stretching out to it. I am not alone. Alice stands to my left, twirling her long black hair around her fingers nervously.

'This feels strange,' I say, my chest fluttering with either excitement or nerves. I can never tell the difference.

'It's nice to be going to the same school.' Alice smiles.

I nod in agreement. Alice and I met when we were five and she moved onto the road I lived on at the time. One of our neighbours had a garden party; and I have faint memories of meeting on the swing set at the bottom of the garden, where dandelions danced gloriously in the breeze. We spent the rest of the summer riding our scooters up and down the road, our mothers chatting as they kept an eye on us. We have been friends ever since.

'I hope everyone is friendly,' I say, as we begin the descent down the path towards the crowd.

We head towards the crowd of children who look about our age. They are forming a queue outside the school hall, all dressed like clones in the same striped navy, green and white uniform. We join the back of the line and I look down at my uniform proudly. The blazer itches, but I feel pleased to be wearing a smart uniform like the children do in the books that I love. Underneath my blazer is a white and green striped blouse. The pattern reminds me of pyjamas, but it certainly doesn't feel like pyjamas. The material is like cardboard against my skin. My eyes scan over my pleated skirt, navy blue and reaching midway down my knee. On my feet are patent Clarks shoes, over white socks fresh out of the Sainsbury's packet. They are not frilled like they were at primary school, because here they cannot be frilly.

Alice and I aren't the back of the queue for long. A girl soon joins the queue behind us. I turn to give her a smile. Her fair blonde hair is swept into a high ponytail, her wide glasses sheltering her eyes from her fringe. My eyes widen as I clock her pink rucksack.

'The rules say we have to have blue backpacks.' I lean over

to warn her, thinking she will thank me. She doesn't. After making a noise I can only describe as a huff, she turns on her heel and marches off towards another group. They stare my way. A feeling of uneasiness spreads through me as I am reminded of Ruth and the girls.

'Did I say something wrong?' I ask Alice, worriedly.

Her mouth opens as if to answer, but she is interrupted by the movement of the queue ahead of us. Voices fall silent as we are led into the school hall. It is huge compared to the one at my primary school, although not as impressive as I had imagined. There are no chandeliers or great long tables like at Hogwarts. Instead, the hall floor is lined with rows of plastic chairs. Ushers guide us into rows. I find myself stuck in the middle. My chest tightens and I wish I was sat nearer the edge.

I stare up at the stage. Giant red curtains hang from the ceiling to the stage's side, framing it in cloth. A lectern is positioned in the middle, the school logo hanging on velvet from it. Behind it, a PowerPoint slide is reflected on the wall. Big bold letters read 'Welcome Year 7s'. *Year* 7, I think. How did that happen? I vividly remember sitting on the carpet on my first day of Year 3, excited for the topics we would be covering that year. It doesn't feel that long ago.

A man wearing a long dark robe that drags on the floor behind him approaches the lectern. He coughs, silencing the hum. Then he begins to speak. His voice is low and croaky, reminding me of Dumbledore from *Harry Potter* – probably only because he is slightly old and grey and *Harry Potter* is the only film I have watched in months. I have it on repeat constantly.

'Welcome, students. It's a pleasure to have you join us. I hope you will take every opportunity offered to you during your time here, to become well-rounded individuals.'

I make a mental note of this, vowing to take up every single opportunity that I am offered.

And so, as the school year begins, I do just that.

I read hundreds of books and win the platinum reading award. I enter the poetry competition and win, though I later consider that I may have been the only participant. I am then asked to write a poem for the Royal Society of Chemistry about my chemistry teacher, which I do. I join book club and attend every author event I can. I even ask our librarian, a kind woman I quickly grow attached to, to invite my favourite authors in – and she does! At the same time, I join netball club, hockey club and dance club. These exhaust me and I dread the days I have them. The PE changing rooms are loud, smelly and cramped. But, my new friends all do them and I don't want to be left out. I like my new friends. I have, without effort, found myself in a group of five, and the other four girls don't seem to judge me like Ruth did. They even join book club with me. I feel incredibly lucky.

One Tuesday afternoon, just after I have finished lunchtime hockey club, I have maths last period. I rush from the changing rooms, pulling my hair out of its ponytail as I run. The familiar feeling of dread settles in the pit of my stomach. I hate maths because my teacher is scary. Usually she is all right to me, because I get on with the work and she can tell that I am clever.

I reach my desk and open my rucksack, pulling out my exercise books and pencil case. Then the realisation hits me, in a stab to my abdomen. I immediately feel sick and my chest and tummy feel funny. I still don't really have a word for what this feeling is, but it is uncomfortable and it makes me want to run away.

I stand behind my desk waiting, tapping my foot restlessly on the floor. Then she appears, dressed in black trousers and a knitted jumper, her grey hair wrapped in a bun. Her presence alone silences the class at once.

'You can sit.' Her hoarse voice rings around the room.

I slide my chair out from under the desk and sit down. My leg bounces up and down, reflecting the pace of my heartbeat. I feel my hand raise in the air and shake, like the rest of my body.

'Yes?' she says, peering at me through her glasses. Her voice is sharp and unkind.

I hesitate, stumbling over my words. 'I'm really sorry . . . I forgot my protractor.'

She stares at me, her eyes boring into me like daggers. 'Well, that isn't okay.'

'I . . . I'm sorry.' Tears begin to slide down my cheeks silently. I imagine my protractor lying on the floor of my bedroom, probably half-tucked under my bed. I had checked my bag twice last night but had still somehow missed it.

My teacher begins to say a lot of other words. Things like 'detention'. Things like 'not good enough'. Things like 'responsibility'.

I have never forgotten anything before for class. I have failed. My breathing begins to get quicker and I am aware of my classmates staring at me. My tears aren't silent anymore, but loud sobs. I rock backwards and forwards in my chair. I know she hasn't stopped, but her voice goes straight through me.

I picture home. My bedroom. Lying on my bed, watching *Harry Potter*. My hamster, Twinkle, is on my lap, chewing on some treats. Mum and Dad are downstairs cooking dinner and my brother and sister are playing together next door. Their laughter echoes around the house. Normally this would bother me. But this time it doesn't because in my mind I am at home and I am safe.

'Are you listening to me?' Her sharp voice cuts through me like ice, making me jump.

I nod, scared to reply in case she tells me I am talking back to her, like adults have before. It never makes sense when adults ask a question and then tell you off for 'answering back', as if you were expected to know you weren't meant to answer, despite them asking in the first place.

She seems to be paying no attention to the fact that I am hysterical. That I am shaking and terrified. She stops telling me off and moves her attention to another boy, who asks to take his blazer off. She says no because it's not hot in here. I think it is hot. So hot, in fact, that I feel suffocated. And it's uncomfortable to work while wearing a blazer. I don't understand how she can tell us that we aren't allowed to take our blazers off.

For the first time, I notice that there is another adult in the room. She leans towards me. She is the lady with mousey-brown hair who doesn't usually talk to the rest of us. She sits next to one of the boys and helps him with his work. Sometimes she takes him out the room when he gets frustrated. But now, she talks to me.

'Take some deep breaths. In, and out, in and out. Stop crying.' Her voice is much softer than the maths teacher's. She has a strange look on her face, one I don't recognise.

I try to do what she says, feeling the rise and fall of my chest. My sobs quieten. As the lesson begins, she continues to look my way to offer reassurance. I don't know if I am getting a detention or not, but I know I'm in trouble. And I hate being in trouble. I try so hard. I didn't mean to forget my protractor.

That evening, I check my bag three times instead of two. It takes longer than it used to and stops me being able to finish *Harry Potter and the Half-Blood Prince.* I hate not finishing a film, but I also hate not going to bed on time. So, I stop the film, but then I am too worked-up to sleep. Knowing that I have to go to maths again tomorrow fills me with dread. I never had this fear of teachers at primary school; and I had never expected to feel this at secondary school, but it quickly becomes a worry that keeps me up at night.

You would think that I would have been the sort of child to have hated the idea of moving to secondary school, considering how much I hate change. But I wasn't. I was excited for school to be more like the schools in the books that I read (spoiler: it wasn't at all), and I couldn't wait to get away from Ruth and the other girls. *And* it meant that I no longer had to go swimming. This was good. I hated (and still hate) swimming – unless it's in a private pool in a villa abroad. I know, I sound like a spoiled brat. But I promise you it is for good autistic reasons, as you will see.

REASONS WHY I HATE SWIMMING POOLS

» Everyone is swimming practically naked in the same water as me, which doesn't feel very clean.
» My body takes too long to adjust to the temperature and my legs come out in heat rashes.
» The smell of chlorine is too strong and gives me a headache.
» I got a verruca from swimming lessons once and I had to go to a chiropodist. And I do not like people touching my feet.
» The water makes my eyes sting.
» Too many people pee in pools.
» My swimming teacher pushed me in when I was ten and made my belly hurt a lot.
» The changing rooms are grubby.

» There is hair everywhere and I hate hair.
» The pool area is too hot.
» And too loud and echoey.
» I feel self-conscious wearing a swimsuit in front of strangers.
» It feels kind of pointless because I am swimming lengths but am not actually going anywhere.

To some extent, I thrived in Year 7. To not have to go swimming removed a lot of stress. I excelled in every subject – as ever, a high achiever. Apart from in art. I found the instructions confusing and my lack of interest in the subject made it hard for me to focus. My art teacher told my parents at parents' evening that I followed her around like a 'lost puppy' asking her questions that she had already explained the answers to. I felt humiliated.

In every other subject, though, I was pretty much a nerd. I thrived on achieving a lot academically and this started to form a big part of what I perceived my identity to be. I know that my academic abilities meant that I was somewhat privileged in the school system. Although I was autistic and undiagnosed, as well as with undiagnosed ADHD, I did not experience the same barriers to learning that many others have. I do not have dyslexia, dyscalculia or dyspraxia. I was not taken out of class in front of my peers for special educational classes – there should not be any embarrassment in this, but I know from other autistic people that there can be. I was never made to feel small by my teachers for my academic ability. I thrived when I was learning. But school was still like navigating a minefield. Or like wading through quicksand that was desperate to suffocate me.

It is hard to explain how difficult a school day can be for an autistic child. Let's walk through a typical school day for me, so you can get an idea of what it took to navigate it. And remember, every autistic child is different. What one finds challenging, another may not.

A SCHOOL DAY

7am – The alarm goes off, but your eyes are so heavy from not sleeping well. You were awake until 2am feeling anxious. Your brain wouldn't switch off.

7.10am – You put on your school uniform, which is itchy, and you know it will irritate your skin all day. The rashes from the day before are still visible on your legs.

8am – You leave for school, heading for the lion's den. Your chest feels tight, but you don't have a choice.

8.30am – You walk into the school grounds. It is loud and busy and feels chaotic.

8.35am – In form time, someone says a joke. You don't laugh because you don't understand it. So, they tell you that you're 'dumb'. You hang your head in shame.

8.55am – The bell rings. It is a screeching noise and it hurts your ears. It takes ten minutes for them to stop hurting.

9am – You are in your first class of the day. Except your normal teacher is off sick and you have a cover teacher. The whole class is messing about, not sitting in the seating plan and being very loud. You feel anxious because everything is different and chaotic. It is not what you expected.

10am – It is the second class of the day. You are already exhausted and your brain is still fixated on the fact that first period wasn't how you expected it to be. At the end of the lesson, you politely remind the teacher that she has forgotten to collect everyone's homework. The class moans at you. You don't understand. You just wanted to make sure you had done your homework properly.

11am – It is breaktime. You follow your friends reluctantly to the canteen and stand in the queue. You are shoved and pushed. You struggle to breathe because everyone is taller than you and you feel suffocated. When you get out of the queue, it is still too loud, too hot and too bright.

11.15am – It is third period. Except this class is in a room which has such a strong smell that you can't concentrate on your work. You ask your friend if they can smell it, but it isn't bothering them. You can't do anything about it, so you wait for the headache to come and pray that it doesn't turn into a migraine.

12.15pm – It is fourth period. Your English teacher announces that she wants to 'mix things up a bit', so has moved all the chairs to the side of the room. She says that you have to work in small groups to create a scene from the play you are studying. You don't say anything to your group, because last time they told you not to be so 'bossy'. But this means your scene isn't prepared in time, so you get kept behind at lunchtime.

1.30pm – Lunchtime was meant to start ten minutes ago, but you got kept behind because your group didn't finish the work. So now everything is out of sync. You don't have time to eat your lunch before your club, so you are hungry for the rest of the day.

1.45pm – It is book club. Your favourite part of the week. You get to sit in the library, which has been closed off to other students. You are meant to talk about books, but everyone else starts talking about different things and the focus on books slips. You're left feeling disappointed.

2.20pm – It is your final class of the day. You struggle to concentrate through it, because your brain is fixated on the book you were studying in book club. You still have three pages left of the chapter and your brain can't stop thinking about that. You end up missing everything your teacher is saying, despite trying very hard to pay attention.

3.45pm – You get home and start on your homework. It's meant to take only a couple of hours, but it takes all evening because you are a perfectionist. You redo your English essay three times because it's not neat enough. Then you have to go over what you did in class because you couldn't focus.

8pm – You have to revise for tomorrow's maths test. You *think* you know what you need to know, but you understand that unless you know *exactly everything* you need to know, your brain won't function during the test. You need to pre-empt the questions and know what to expect or anxiety will take over.

9.30pm – You pack your school bag for the next day. You check it to make sure you have remembered

everything, including your protractor. Then you
check again. And again.

10pm – You head to bed, exhausted. There was no
time to read this evening, or watch any TV. Now
you lie awake for hours, your brain refusing to
switch off.

Experiencing this stress day after day can be very damaging
to an autistic child. Though, of course, every autistic child
experiences school differently. And it's worth remembering
that those with learning difficulties like dyslexia or co-
occurring conditions like ADHD might have additional
challenges or different experiences too. These experiences
can be traumatising. I was, in some ways, lucky, because my
perfectionism, studiousness and love for learning gave me an
advantage that other neurodivergent students may not have.
I was never perceived to be 'naughty' or 'disruptive' like many
are, even when they aren't in control of their bodies not sitting
still or their brains not concentrating. I managed to fly under
the radar, praised for my academic abilities, until I could no
longer contain my anxiety.

I don't think many autistic children get through school
untraumatised – and that is incredibly sad. Because being
forced into an environment that does not cater for the way
your brain works day after day – an environment of loud
noise, chaos, and bright lights that makes you want to rip your
skin off – and not having a choice about it, is traumatising.
Especially if you are then told repeatedly that you just have to
deal with it, while the noise of the classroom physically hurts
your ears. This environment can trigger horrific meltdowns;
yet the child is then forced back into that same environment
the next day, as if the outcome will somehow be different.

Autistic children learn that they have to withstand pain, that it is okay for them to be in physical and emotional pain and that their needs don't matter. This doesn't set them up well for enforcing boundaries later in life.

Autistic children deserve the chance to thrive and I hope that our generation can be a part of making that happen.

It is a drizzly Monday afternoon. Grey clouds swarm angrily in the sky, sending raindrops catapulting to the ground. They turn the grass glossy and the pavement mahogany. I stare out of the murky window, past the splatters that blur my view, to the space outside the undercover seating area. Water drips from the drainpipes, sploshing into puddles forming on the pavement. Remains of crumbs from lunchtime soak through, turning into mush.

I am seated on a stool, the metal legs cold against my bare legs. It is nearing winter, but I am still insistent that I will not wear tights until the weather gives me no choice. In this classroom, though, I almost regret my decision. Despite the windows being closed, the biology labs are freezing. The building is old, with thin walls and loose window seals. I can feel the draught from my seat.

My thoughts, far away from the alleles and twin studies we are meant to be looking at, are quickly diverted, as a clatter of chairs steals my attention. My neck whips to my left, catching sight of one of the boys rocking on the floor beside his bench. His hands grip onto his knees, his body swaying backwards and forwards. I don't know who he is. Our class has been mixed with different year groups today, because there are too many teachers off sick.

'Come on. Let's go to the support base.' The lady with brown hair, who I now smile at whenever we pass by each other, crouches on the floor beside him. She must work with him too. She has been trying to take him outside before he escalates, but he is refusing to go with her.

'Leave. Me. Alone!' he shouts, his hands gripping his ears. He makes noises which sound like he is distressed. I want to put my hands over my ears too.

The lady leans closer to him, talking softly in his ear. The whole class is staring at her. I don't even realise until afterwards that perhaps this isn't the most sensitive thing to do. But no one tells us not to. Our class teacher has rushed out the classroom, presumably to call someone.

The brown-haired woman's words evidently don't help, as suddenly the boy lashes out with his arms. He narrowly misses her, but she is taken by surprise and stumbles backwards, nearly tripping. She manages to steady herself, leaning onto the cupboard for stability. He has grabbed hold of his stool, holding it out in front of him. I am not sure if this is as a weapon or a defence.

'Breathe, just breathe,' she says, her voice now shaking in trepidation.

'NO!' he shouts, lifting the stool above his head. He throws it at the wall with force. It smacks the display of essays and then crashes loudly onto the floor.

He lifts another stool just as the assistant headteacher arrives at the door. She asks us all to leave the room quietly, row by row. The boy stares at us. His eyes are bloodshot and he is trembling. I think that he looks angry. Or maybe he is just scared.

We are ushered to the library and our teacher continues the lesson there, like nothing has happened. She ignores the whispers. I can't, though. It's an underlying murmur, making it impossible to concentrate. I catch Max, from my form group, saying that the boy probably just put it on to get out of class.

His friend Jared says that he shouldn't be at our school if he is going to be violent. Someone else says that it's unfair our learning got disrupted and he won't even get into trouble because he's 'on the spectrum'. I wonder how they know that. It makes anger begin to bubble inside of me, like lava in a volcano preparing to erupt. My cousin also has autism and finds it hard to cope at school. I don't say anything because we are not meant to be talking. I just let the anger fester.

At breaktime on Wednesday, I am grabbing my French textbook from my locker when I overhear a conversation. Max is leaning on one of the lockers, his mobile phone in his hand. He would have it confiscated if the teacher saw.

'He's been expelled, I heard,' Max says, a grin spreading across his face.

'That's good. We would be if we threw a chair across the room,' Jared replies, checking his gelled hair in the reflection of the window.

I slam my locker shut and turn to them, hand on my hip. 'That's rubbish. He won't be expelled. He probably just needs some time to recover.'

Max, red-cheeked, sniggers. 'Recover from what?'

'How he felt?' I scrunch up my nose in distaste, realising that I have no interest in talking to either of them.

This time they both snigger. I roll my eyes and walk away, feeling fury at their immaturity.

Our last lesson that day is supposed to be art, but our art teacher tells us that we are having an assembly. This throws me. We never have assemblies during lessons. But at least I get to miss art, I suppose.

We trek to the school hall and silently file into the chairs row by row. There are a couple of teachers sat on the stage.

I briefly wonder if someone has died. What could they possibly want to talk to multiple year groups about? I notice Mrs J, the Special Educational Needs Co-ordinator (SENCo), fiddling with the computer screen, trying to get the projector to work. Most of us haven't met her before. But I've seen her around school. She's a middle-aged lady whose hair is just starting to turn grey at the roots. She wears flowery dresses that trawl along the ground as she walks. She has one of those auras that makes me feel comfortable immediately.

A PowerPoint presentation flicks onto the wall, the projector finally working. The slide is titled 'Autism Spectrum Disorder'. When the last class has sat down and there is silence, she gives a slight cough and begins to speak.

'Hello everyone. Sorry to have pulled you out of your last lesson, but we wanted to talk to you about something because we would like you all to have a better understanding. As you can probably tell from the PowerPoint, that is autism.'

She spends the next 45 minutes teaching us about it. She tells us about how sounds can be painful for people with autism, how understanding and regulating emotions can be tricky and how social situations can be overwhelming. I listen intently, and notice that, surprisingly, Max and Jared seem to be listening too. In fact, most people are. As I listen, I consider how overwhelming things can get for me and I wonder how overwhelming it must be for those with autism, like my cousin. If *I* find noise difficult, it must be so much worse for them.

Once the PowerPoint is finished, Mrs J asks if anyone has any questions. One of the girls from the year above puts her hand up, leaning forwards in her seat.

'Yes, Marie?' Mrs J gestures at her.

'How do we know if people have autism and what should we do to help them?' Marie asks, spinning a pen between her fingers. Her voice echoes around the hall.

'That's a good question, Marie. You might not always know unless they tell you or unless your form tutor tells you with their permission. But if you recognise that someone is struggling with any of the things we have discussed, it is important to try and be understanding of that. And if you see people on their own, chat to them. What do you think?'

'That sounds like a good idea.' Marie nods solemnly.

The gentleness in Mrs J's face suddenly evaporates and her voice turns colder.

'I have heard some people say some incorrect things about autism and some of you even use it as an insult. That is to stop. You now all know what autism is, and that means you know better. Any further misinformation or mocking and you will be reprimanded for it. You all need to look out for one another.'

I find myself nodding, remembering what I had heard Max say the other day. I wonder if what happened with that boy has triggered the assembly. I hope he is okay. I haven't seen him around school since. Our paths don't cross, but I know a boy from my English class who is often on his own. I decide that I will keep an eye out for him from now on.

The bell rings, signalling the end of the day. As always, I resist the urge to cover my ears with my hands, waiting instead for the ringing to stop. I find myself behind Max as we leave the assembly, heading out of the hall.

'So, what did you think, then?' I ask, raising an eyebrow, preparing for an immature response. But he surprises me.

'I didn't know autism was like that. Must be hard.' He shrugs, appearing thoughtful. 'Maybe I shouldn't have said what I said.'

I am taken aback. I watch him walk over to the buses, wondering if I had judged him too soon.

The next day, I notice the boy from my English class sat by

himself on the bench by the science block. His dark locks draw his face like curtains, forming a shield that allows him to focus on his notepad. He holds it in his hand, scrawling intently. I almost don't want to interrupt him, but I decide to.

'Hey. How are you?' I ask before taking a bite of my apple. It's a Gala apple – the only type I begrudgingly agree to have. I grimace as the sweetness stings my tastebuds. I tense for the second bite, but this one just fills my mouth with water. That's what I dislike about fruit: the unpredictability, never knowing if each bite will be too sweet, too sour, or just right.

He looks up, and it takes him a moment to register my question. He shuffles awkwardly in his seat. 'I'm good, thank you.'

'Good,' I reply. Then I stand there awkwardly, not knowing what to say next. I take another bite of my apple. Thankfully, he speaks.

'Do you like writing?'

'I do! I love writing stories.' My current writing project is a book about a witch and an angel who fall in love and run away, because witches and angels aren't allowed to be together. Alice has started reading it and I am pleased because she is enjoying it and she doesn't usually like to read.

'Me too! Look at all the stories I've got here,' he says, excitedly showing me his notebook. He hands it to me, to hold. I flick through it gently, careful not to crease the pages. His writing is hard to read. I can make out odd words but not sentences.

'What are they about?' I ask curiously.

'Dragons, mainly. I love dragons. And knights. Anything mythical.'

'That's awesome.'

He grins at me. His dimples shine, and his face doesn't

appear so forlorn. I think it is the first time I have seen him smile.

It is not that hard to make an autistic child's day at school better than it would have been. That may be by educating their class with their permission (a whole-school assembly might be a *little* too much if it appears specific to a person or situation), by connecting them with peers with similar interests, or by encouraging them to use their special interests to help them to thrive.[1] Really, all children should be taught about difference, neurodiversity and disability as soon as they start school, at a level they can understand. Acceptance starts young. But, acceptance is not all that is needed. Adaptations and adjustments are necessary too.

Under the Equality Act 2010,[2] schools have a duty to make reasonable adjustments for anyone with additional needs or disabilities. But an official diagnosis is not required for these adjustments to be put in place, because they are based on need.

It can be hard to know what to ask for or what individuals are entitled to. Here are some reasonable adjustments that schools can put in place.

REASONABLE ADJUSTMENTS AT SCHOOL

» Regular mentoring sessions with a trusted teacher or SENCo.
» Time-out card to leave lessons when needed.
» For exams: a small room, extra time, rest breaks.
» Permission to use fidget toys in class.
» Seating plans catering to the child's needs – for example, being able to sit next to the door or with a friend.

» Movement breaks or 'brain breaks'.
» Uniform adjustments to cater for sensory needs – for example, wearing leggings instead of tights, or not having to wear a tie.
» Extensions on homework when required.
» Reduced timetable to make it more manageable.
» Not having to participate in off-timetable days like school activities if too much.
» Being able to sit in the library when lessons are too much.
» Not having to go to assemblies if they are overwhelming.
» Being able to miss lessons that present unmanageable sensory challenges, such as PE or music.
» Permission to use phone to text a parent or listen to music when needed.
» Notice given of any changes, such as to lesson structures, scheduled 'surprise' tests or teacher replacements.
» New yearly timetables being given as early as possible.

School can be a horrific place for autistic children and young people. We are often under constant stress and constant overload. We must work on making our schools as autism-friendly as possible, because we deserve the same chance as our non-autistic peers to thrive. We need the adjustments to put us on an even playing field. Not having them can be detrimental to both our learning and our mental health.

CHAPTER FIVE

'There is no easy way from the earth to the stars.'
—*Seneca*

The waves pound the shore and a deep fog sits on the horizon. The sky above is filled with angry clouds, circling over our heads like dark predators. It is the start of October half-term and I am stood on the beach in the middle of an oncoming storm. Every year, for as long as I can remember, my grandparents have taken our whole extended family to Devon. We stay in a quaint little village called Hope Cove, which comes to life during the holidays. It is littered with candyfloss-pink and baby-blue cottages, but ours are tucked away in a little nook at the base of a hill. This village has yet to become the tourist attraction it will be later, and our family is starting to be well-known among the local pub and café owners. We return here year after year, spending every day on the beach, the adults chatting to the locals and travellers, my younger cousins competing with the waves to build dams.

I'm not usually the last one on the beach, but today I am.

I hop along the bank of sand, my pink wellies squelching with each step. A gust of wind blows right through me and I stumble, nearly toppling over. It makes me laugh. Briefly, I wish I was wearing a coat, but after the argument I had an hour ago with Mum and Dad because I refused to put one on, I don't let myself entertain the thought a moment longer. My coat is puffy, itchy. It restricts my movement too much and wearing it makes me feel trapped. In just a fleece, I feel freer. I am wearing my stripy pink and orange fleece that I bring each year. I rebuff the idea that it is getting too short. I will wear it for as long as I can.

I stare up over the cliff, at the café. The lights from inside shine over us like headlights. My parents, gran and cousins must be in there, all wrapped up and cosy by the fire. I imagine they are sipping warm tea or hot chocolate with marshmallows and devouring the usual scones with clotted cream and jam. Arguing over whether cream or jam should be on top. My mouth waters at the image. Usually, I am the first one up there, nestled by the fire with a novel in my hand. I have already read four of my books this week and I am savouring my last, in case there aren't any to purchase in Kingsbridge tomorrow.

Grandpa is here on the beach with me. With each Devon trip, the creases on his face grow in number, but each one makes him seem wiser. He is slightly ahead, using his umbrella like a walking stick, poking it into the sand with every step. He says the umbrella is in case it rains, that he doesn't need a walking stick, but I can see that it helps to guide and steady him.

'Hey Emily!' he shouts at me over the whistling of the wind. It sounds like it is talking to itself. 'Do you know what type of cliff that is?'

He points at the jagged clifftop hanging over the murky water. I tilt my head, pretending to ponder over his question. The cliff shape almost looks like a face, its nose protruding out to sea. A layer of white covers the top of it like chalk. After an adequate amount of time, I shake my head, looking at him expectantly. But he only laughs, softly.

'I'm not sure either!'

'Grandpaaa!' I moan, pressing my feet into the sand harder with frustration.

He waits for me to catch up with him, then we walk side by side, our footprints marking our path behind us. He asks me whether I like geography at school and I tell him that I do, even though I'm not sure. I don't want to disappoint him, but I am not finding tectonic plates very captivating.

'Your uncle studied it at university, you know. It's a very good subject to get into. There is much to learn about our earth.'

I nod, knowing that he is wise.

Just as I realise that there is not another person in sight, I feel a hard splatter against my cheek. I sense that a torrent of rain is about to soak us. Sure enough, moments later, the heavens open. My fleece offers little protection. My skin is wet almost instantly.

Grandpa gestures to the steps leading up to the road and begins to hobble in that direction, struggling to open the umbrella. I could run, but I stay close to him, gripping onto his arm as if to steady myself in the wind. I take one last look at the sea as it fights the ever-changing waves, and then head to seek out the warmth.

We make it to the café, soaked through. Grandpa ducks his head under the low doorway. My auntie catches sight of us, immediately standing up from her chair and bustling over to us with a towel from her beach bag.

'Oh look at you two!' She inhales, studying our dripping clothes. I shrug my fleece off and hand it to her. She wraps it into a bundle and places it into her bag. My leggings and T-shirt are still stuck to my skin, my leggings pinching my thighs. I squirm uncomfortably.

'I don't like it!' I jump up and down, shuddering.

Mum walks over, a mug of steaming tea in her hand. 'What did you expect? You could see the rain was coming!'

'It was nice down there,' I mutter, wrapping my auntie's towel around my shoulders and following Grandpa to the table everyone is sat at. Grannie is in the corner, a magazine on her lap, a slice of Victoria sponge on her plate.

'Cake instead of scones?' Grandpa raises an eyebrow.

'I fancied a change!' Grannie chuckles.

Jessica and my cousin Rosie slide down the bench and I squeeze in. My other cousin, Megan, passes me a spare hot chocolate – they ordered too many – and I take a sip, the heat burning my lips. I don't like hot drinks because drinks shouldn't be hot. But I need something to warm me through and I enjoy the sweetness of the marshmallows in my mouth.

'Coffee, Dad?' My auntie taps Grandpa's arm.

'Oh, yes please. One can never have enough coffee!' He winks at me. I grin back at him.

Many of our Devon holidays merge into one long memory in my mind, like one neverending trip. Filled with hours of laughter – and also bickering.

Now it is May 2015. And we are in Hope Cove without my grandpa, my mum and my auntie. They are back in Hertfordshire because Grandpa is in hospital. He has been there for a few weeks now, in bed number three on Bluebell Ward – but it's okay, they say, because he only has a bad back. He is there for physiotherapy and then he will be home, we've been told. He is, or was, very physically well and healthy for his age. Except now he can't move on his own. One of the nurses is meant to help him move every day but Mum says he has been lying flat on his back for weeks. They are short staffed, she says.

But I don't worry, because we have been told he will be okay. And I believe them.

Then, one afternoon, I am in my bedroom in our cottage. The same bedroom I have returned to every year for the past decade. It has a specific smell – kind of musty, the smell of oldness mixed with sand and sea. I am putting away my new make-up that I purchased from Salcombe yesterday. I am learning which shade matches my skin, and what colours complement my complexion. I don't care very much about it, but I don't really like the way I look and the cool girls at school are all into make-up, so I want to try it out too. It has been three years since I last saw Ruth, but sometimes her voice still rings around my head. I have seen on Instagram that she wears a lot of make-up.

The weather outside is miserable, so I am contemplating what DVD I should put on – *The Sound of Music* or *The Cheetah Girls* – wondering which my younger cousins would prefer, when Dad knocks on my door. A soft tap against the wood.

'Come in!' I call out, brightly. I sweep remains of eye shadow into my cupped hand and shake it into the bin.

I expect Dad to speak, but he doesn't, so I turn to face him. He is ashen-faced; I have never seen him look so white. His face crumples and I feel a stab in the pit of my stomach, even before he tells me.

'He's gone, sweetie.'

That is when I learn the meaning of the phrase 'my whole body sank'.

'Whaa . . . what?' I croak.

'Grandpa's passed away.'

He pulls me into a tight hug. I try to move, but he holds me firmer, the pressure helping me to stay grounded. My head is spinning and I think I am going to throw up. Suddenly everything around me doesn't feel real and it is like I am dreaming. It doesn't make sense. He can't have died. I only saw him the other day. He was telling me about being a child during the war, of child evacuees coming to their country village. He was helping me with my history homework. He only has a bad back. I didn't think that a bad back could kill you.

Later that day, I hear the phrase 'hospital-acquired pneumonia', which was the cause of his death. I don't understand how a place that was meant to have helped him and kept him safe effectively killed him.

I first learned that life was not permanent on 7 March 2012. My hamster, Twinkle, had been on the table in front of me, trying to stand up and falling over every time with a whimper. Rufus, the vet, leaned over her. A man our family knew well, having been my grannie's vet of choice for 20 years. He asked me a question and in that moment, death changed from being something I only read about in stories to being right in front of me.

'Are you ready to say goodbye, sweetie?' Dad, standing next to me, repeated Rufus's words.

I blinked back tears, not wanting to cry. Ruth had told me that crying was babyish.

'What's . . . what's going to happen?' I attempted to swallow the lump in the back of my throat.

'I'm going to give her a little injection to make her go to sleep. She won't feel any pain,' Rufus said.

I touched her fur with two fingers. She felt soft and her black beady eyes stared back at me helplessly. I whispered a goodbye and nodded at Rufus. He picked her up and carried her out of the room. I understood I wouldn't see her alive again, but I wondered how come he was allowed to decide her life was over, just like that.

'Daddy. If Grannie was very ill like Twinkle, would her doctor put her down too?'

'It doesn't quite work like that.' He looked at me, wearily. His glasses were slightly steamed.

'Why not? What if she was in even more pain than Twinkle?'

'We'll talk about it later.' He placed his hand on my shoulder. It was meant to be a reassuring gesture, but then Rufus returned with Twinkle's limp body tucked up beneath her bedding in a small box and I recoiled. I didn't want to be touched.

As with many (arguably, lucky) children, losing my first pet was the first time that I was forced to confront death. Then I was asked if I wanted to get another hamster (on the same day – which was rather inconsiderate of my mother, I thought!). Not long after, I did. She looked pretty much identical to Twinkle (though don't all hamsters look alike?). I named her Mango. And, I began to wonder, if I could replace Twinkle that fast, could people be replaced too?

When I lost my grandfather a couple of years later, I was reminded of Twinkle dying. But this time, I couldn't get a new grandfather. And I didn't want a new grandfather. I wanted mine.

Except he was gone – and understanding the permanence of the situation was something I really struggled to process. As each day passed, I found this increasingly troubling.

Around me, everyone else was upset, devastated, but they seemed, somehow, to keep going.

I internalised what I was feeling, trying to make sense of it. I spent a lot of time thinking at first. I don't think I cried very much. But I remember clearly that I began to worry that every time I said goodbye to someone I loved, I wouldn't see them again. This clouded my mind.

The weeks following his death were confusing and overwhelming. But, as the eldest of three siblings and the eldest of seven cousins, I had a role to play. I tried to help with preparations with the funeral, though became overly fixated on a poem I wanted to read at the service and had a terrible meltdown when my uncle was chosen to read it instead.

On another occasion, I tried to comfort my mum, but then found myself feeling extremely awkward in the emotional situation and so I left the room because I didn't know how to act.

I dutifully led the line of the cousins walking down the aisle at the funeral with balloons, then fainted afterwards, likely from overwhelm, but I didn't know that at the time. I just felt completely out of my depth.

I tried to talk to the people my grandmother wanted me to at the wake, then hid in the corner on my phone because it was just all too much, too confusing, too many emotions and sensations to deal with.

Of course, no one knew I was autistic at the time, and in the days immediately following my grandpa's death, my emotional reaction might not have been very different to that of many non-autistic children coping with grief. But now I realise that my mind was finding this life-changing situation incredibly difficult to process, and I was unconsciously making an enormous effort to mask much of my confusion and the emotional turmoil I felt inside.

The full extent of the impact of this loss, the emotional and mental confusion it triggered within me, had not yet revealed itself.

For other autistic children, the immediate aftermath of a loss can be even more difficult[1] than it was for me.

The good news is, there are things that can help autistic children to navigate loss and grief.

WHAT MAY HELP AN AUTISTIC CHILD (OR ANY CHILD!) NAVIGATE LOSS

» Prepare them with clear language. This is less confusing for them. Instead of 'Uncle Albert isn't very well', say, 'Uncle Albert has __ and doesn't have long to live.'

» Explain what may happen if the person in question does die and what the child should expect to happen.

» Explain what this will mean for them – for example, a change of routine or activities because the person is no longer present.

» Talk about it, as much as they want to.

» When the person dies, state this clearly without using euphemisms. Don't say, 'They have gone', say 'They have died'. This can prevent a lot of confusion.

» Some children do need to know exactly what has happened – don't tell them the person just had a poorly tummy or head, because this may make them think they will die if they have a sore head or tummy.

» Help them to understand that this is permanent.

» Accept that they may process or display grief differently, and that that is okay.

» Visit the funeral site or burial ground in advance if possible.

» Ensure there is someone available for them if they have any questions about death.

» Help them to remember the person through photographs, videos or belongings.

It is important to remember that some autistic people may display grief in untypical ways. For example, through aggression, or delayed reactions, or even by displaying 'inappropriate' responses like not appearing sad. This could be hard for people around them to navigate. It is important to understand that just because someone's grief reaction is different to yours, it doesn't make it wrong. We all grieve differently.

It's often not just the loss that can be difficult, but also the loss of routine that comes with it. This is the case for many people when they lose someone they love, but for autistic people, whose brains rely so heavily on routine and familiarity, it can be even more challenging. I no longer came home on Wednesday afternoons to Grandpa standing at the kitchen table, newspaper in hand, ready to show me a particular page that he had folded in anticipation of my arrival. Sometimes this story was about something dreadful that had happened overseas; other times it was simply a local story about a dogwalker finding a missing cat. It stopped being 'Grannie and Grandpa' and started being just 'Grannie'. Our annual trips to Devon, which anchored me in a way I can't explain, were no longer the same. It was all different. And I didn't cope very well with the change.

Coping with loss is something that nobody ever teaches you how to do. It is something which just happens, often unexpectedly, that you just have to learn to deal with. Because there is no guidebook and no magic cure for grief.

HOW TO COPE WITH THE LOSS OF SOMEONE YOU LOVE

» Cry.
» Cry some more.
» Cry a lot more.
» Eat some chocolate.
» Talk to the person you have lost.
» Life will get busy again – let it.

» Pray.
» Write a letter to the person.
» There will be a day you won't cry – that's okay.
» Allow time.
» Allow some more time.
» Some days will pass when you think of them less – that's okay.
» Allow even more time.
» Talk about them with others who loved them.
» Eat some more chocolate.
» Think about what they would say to you now.
» Look at photos and videos.
» Make them proud of you.
» Know that one day, life won't feel as painful as it feels right now.

It took a long time for me to process what had happened and to understand that I wouldn't see my grandpa again. He was a good man. He taught me a lot about the world, and I am incredibly grateful to have had him in my life for the 13 years that I did. I only wish it could have been longer. I wish he could have seen me grow up just a little bit more before he had to leave.

Grandpa made the concept of death – something that only happened in the books that I read, and that seemed so distant and seemingly unreal – real. To me, he had seemed completely fine one day, yet was dead the next. He made it known to me that the same thing could happen to other people I loved too. And from that moment on, I could never be sure when seeing a loved one if it would be the last time.

I couldn't understand (and still struggle to, like many people do, I'm sure) how a person could be alive, breathing, stood right in front of you one day, and nowhere to be seen on earth the next. How their heart could just stop beating, sometimes with no warning whatsoever. I know too many good people who have died, and each time their death has made the world feel a little less safe to live in.

When Grandpa died, I had no choice but to begin to learn to cope with his loss and the change that came with it. Although, as time went on, I would realise that losing him set into motion a series of events that would change the course of my teenage years. Because, merely weeks after his death, reality as I knew it began to shift dangerously.

CHAPTER SIX

'Without fear there cannot be courage.'
—Christopher Paolini

I believe that, for most autistic people, there is a point when living in a world that caters wholly for neurotypical people and ostracises autistic people breaks you. When working ten times harder than everyone else to get through each day because you have a different neurotype is too exhausting to maintain.

For many, that comes in the form of mental health difficulties.

It is no surprise that research has shown that 80 per cent of autistic people experience mental health problems at some stage in their lives, the most prevalent being depression and anxiety.[1]

I don't even know how you begin to disentangle anxiety and autism in our current world. Constantly balancing routine, emotions and the scales of anxiety requires a huge amount of effort, in order to avoid uncontrollable meltdowns or panic attacks that render us exhausted.

It is no wonder so many autistic people have anxiety, when our minds thrive on things the world does not offer, like predictability, routine and literality. Nor that so many have depression, when the world constantly shouts at us that we don't deserve to be accepted for who we are. Nor that so many have eating disorders, when bullying and trauma make us hate ourselves and we seek control over a world that feels so *out* of control.

This is the point at which I began to break.

I am 13 and in Belgium, on a school history trip. In the past 24 hours, we have visited more cemeteries and memorials than I have ever even seen on television. Now we are at the Menin Gate Memorial, in Ypres. It is shaped in a magnificent arch, towering above us. The arch blocks out some of the sunlight; it's almost as if the dimness is more respectful to the thousands honoured here. Some light gets in through a cavity in the ceiling, illuminating the names etched into the wall.

Outside, there is little shade and it is baking hot under the direct sun – it must be in the late twenties. I am grateful to be shaded for now, but my skin is still sticky and itchy from sweat. There are too many people around me, moving about in groups like swarms of bees. There is even a buzz, despite us having been warned to be quiet.

I am silent, though. My friends have already made their way out from the arch, I think to the grass that lines the road outside. But I am still standing, staring at the wall. My eyes dart from name to name. There are thousands: 54,395 to be precise.* All soldiers who died in one of the battles in World War One but who have no known graves. They passed right through the road I am standing on, on their way to battle. This thought makes me feel queasy. All of the names I am looking

---

* This was the number at the time of my visit but it is continually adjusted over time as more names are added or removed when remains are recovered.

at represent individuals with families, hobbies, relationships and lives. All of them had people who loved them.

An image of Grandpa pops into my head. I am standing in the hallway of Grannie and Grandpa's house. It is a fairly grand house. With lots of photo frames hanging from the walls and decorations collected from the numerous trips they have taken in their lifetime. It is the sort of house that definitely belongs to someone's grandparents – it just so happens to be mine. A key turns in the front door and he steps onto the deep green carpet, armed with two plastic bags. He's slightly out of breath and his wrinkly cheeks are rosy red. He is dressed in his usual beige trousers and blue sweater, his watch a shiny gold on his wrist.

'Did you get the ice cream?' my cousin Rosie asks, bounding over to him. She is wearing a little black dress covered in poppies. Grannie bought it for her from a market stall.

'Yes, yes,' he mumbles. 'Let me get through the door.'

Rosie claps her hands gleefully, twirling on the spot. Grandpa edges around her and into the kitchen, where he places the shopping bags on the countertop. He lifts the tub of ice cream out of one of them and grabs four bowls from the cupboard.

'Do you want to serve it, Emily?' He hands a spoon to me. I have not served ice cream before. I do not know if I am strong enough. I prise the lid off the tub with my hands, feeling the plastic dig into my skin. The ice cream is frozen solid against the spoon.

Grannie passes through the kitchen, a crate of laundry in her arms. I feel her peer over my shoulder, her rosy perfume wafting up my nose.

'You might have to wait a couple of minutes for it to get softer,' she suggests.

'Oww,' Rosie moans, hitting her head with her palm.

'I'll do it,' Grandpa says, pulling the tub towards him. 'We don't want you to have to wait, do we!'

I lift Rosie into my arms, and we watch as he manages to scoop the ice cream into four portions. Strawberry, vanilla and chocolate, all mixed together. Our mouths water.

I smile. 'Thank you, Grandpa.'

The memory fades out and I am brought back to the present. It is only a month since he passed away. Suddenly, my head begins to feel fuzzy and my vision blurs. I struggle to catch my breath, which is strange. I look to my side for reassurance, then remember that my friends are not with me. I am surrounded by kids in my year who I barely know.

I push through the crowds, out of the arch. The sun is blazing hot on my face, the temperature of fire. I can't see very well, but I know that I need to find a teacher. For a reason unbeknown to me, light tears brush against my cheeks. My breath doesn't feel like it is in my control. I can't quite catch it. Briefly, I wonder if I am having a heart attack.

My eyes land on my history teacher. I am soon safe, but I can't breathe. The noise around me pierces my ears. My teacher is leaning towards me; her mouth is moving. But the noise is all jumbled up and I cannot make out the sounds. She sounds so far away. I crumple to the floor, hands gripping onto my ears.

This must be it. I must be dying, I think. Then my surroundings fade to black.

Later that day, I am lying on a single hospital bed in a small room, with a cannula in my arm. I am connected to a machine that beeps every so often, which irritates me. My legs are covered in bright-red rashes and my breathing is still hasty and raspy. I have been given an oxygen mask to breathe into, but it makes my throat clog up more; it is too claustrophobic.

Staff bustle past the door, speaking in a foreign language, and I remember I am in Belgium. My parents aren't here. Instead, to the left of my bed, my history teacher is sat on a plastic chair. She is flicking through a children's book, ignoring the Dutch text. Instead, she is making up the story by the pictures.

'Dolly goes to the shop to buy a baguette, but Dolly isn't happy,' she says, staring at an image of a little girl holding a bread roll at the supermarket. I'm not sure why she thinks she doesn't look happy; her expression looks neutral to me. 'Then Dolly goes home.'

'Miss! This is stupid!' I moan, hitting my forehead with my palm.

'You got any other idea to pass the time?' She raises an eyebrow at me, and my lips turn into a smile.

I have always loved my history teacher. She has a defining presence about her, of gentleness but also authoritativeness. Apart from her insistence that our skirts aren't rolled up, she is patient and overly caring. The sort of teacher that sometimes acts a bit more like your mum than a teacher, while still passionately imparting knowledge about her subject in any way that she can. She is wise, I know that for certain, and I admire her.

Just as we reach the end of the story, a nurse comes into the room. She proceeds to take out my cannula. She doesn't say much else. They have already established that I had a panic attack, which seemed to have caused heat rashes on my legs and pins and needles spiralling through my hands and feet. I don't understand why; I've never had a panic attack before. But they don't explain why it might have happened. They just say that I can leave soon, once my blood-test results come back. I don't want to head back to the hostel anyway – it is too hot and busy there; it makes me feel ill. And I am worried it will happen again. I don't know how I would stop it.

'Are you okay?' the nurse asks with a heavy accent.

I ignore the knot in my stomach and nod. I don't know when the knot will go away.

When we arrive back at the hostel, the panic does overwhelm me again – and again I think that I am dying. This happens multiple times a day over the following two days of the trip. Each time, the weariness in the teachers' voices grows. I know I am being a pain; I don't know what is wrong with me. I'm frightened. My body is overwhelmed by the different feelings and the exhaustion that each attack leaves me subjected to. And there is no time to decompress because we head from destination to destination, from memorial to grave to cemetery and back again.

I tell myself that it is only temporary because I will be home soon. And when I am home, I will feel safe. Back in familiarity and comfort. Away from the reminder of death.

But, it turns out, things don't go like that. At home, the panic attacks continue. With each attack, I feel more frustrated and angry with myself. I also feel more reluctant to go outside, and more afraid it will happen again. Each time I lose control, I feel like I am suffocating. I am too scared to be alone in case it happens and I collapse and don't wake up. But being around people is also too exhausting. My body is in a permanent state of recovery; each time my energy returns, another panic attack rips it out of me.

During the next two weeks at school, before the end of the summer term, my anxiety is constant and severe. I no longer move from lesson to lesson, hidden in the sea of children. I rush out of lessons, I hide under desks rocking and struggling to breathe, I refuse to go to lessons and stay in the library. I have learned that when I force myself to do things, I invite panic attacks.

I don't know what has happened to me, but I am scared, frozen and trapped.

In 1897, a US physiologist named Walter Cannon was studying digestive mechanisms in animals when he noticed something interesting.[2] Namely, that there were accompanying changes in the digestive system of animals who appeared scared or stressed. Peristalsis, the contractions that enable food to move from the mouth to the stomach, would slow or sometimes even cease. This intrigued him enough to begin to study all of the physiological responses that animals have to stress.

Both animals and humans have what is called an autonomic nervous system. This is part of the peripheral nervous system, and regulates physiological processes such as blood pressure, digestion and heart rate.[3] It is made up of two parts – the sympathetic nervous system and the parasympathetic nervous system. I am not entirely sure why they have those names – I wouldn't say they are very sympathetic at all.

After over a decade of investigations, in 1915, Cannon published his results.[4] He demonstrated that when an animal is stressed, their sympathetic nervous system is activated and releases adrenaline to prepare them for response. He called this the 'fight-or-flight' response.

The same thing can be seen in humans. When a person's brain perceives there to be a potential threat, it prepares us for action in order to keep us safe. We can either 'fight' it or run away in a 'flight' response. Our sympathetic nervous system increases our heart rate, sends blood to our muscles, releases hormones like adrenaline and activates our sweat glands, as well as slowing down energy-wasting functions such as digestion to better prepare us for action.

This system is meant to protect us. It helped our ancestors stay safe from predators.

But what happens when this same system triggers unnecessary panic?

In this case, our fight-or-flight system is inappropriately activated. Our sympathetic nervous system is still triggered. We experience all of the symptoms of panic, as if we are standing in front of a predator, when there is no real risk. And this can be suffocating.

This was the explanation that I was given, over and over, about why I was experiencing panic attacks. I imagined myself as a caveman, standing in a barren desert in front of a lion. And all I could think about was that I would never have survived. Because my panic attacks left me shaking on the ground, unable to move. A prime target.

Perhaps my reactions were better explained by the 'freeze' reaction, a third response later added to the fight-or-flight theory.[5] There was an argument that this response had some value, since 'playing dead' may enable you to hide from predators. Unfortunately, if I was being pursued by a sabre-toothed tiger, I think the shaking and noise from my hyperventilating would have given me away.

At the time, I did not know that whatever was happening inside my brain was linked to autism. I couldn't understand where all the anxiety had come from. The feeling of initial anxiety was familiar – so familiar that I couldn't pinpoint exactly when it had first started – but I wasn't used to its growing intensity and the panic attacks that ensued.

When that first panic attack hit, I had no idea that it would mark the beginning of a major battle. I had no idea that I would spend the next few years of my life a prisoner to panic. I also had no idea that overnight I would change from a golden child, who teachers loved to have in the classroom, to a child teachers had to battle with just to get them to sit in class and who would end up disrupting the lesson once the panic took hold.

Anything could cause it, but noise, crowds, strangers, changes to routine or thoughts of death or danger were common triggers.

You see, my brain had essentially reached boiling point. A switch had been flicked. Thirteen years of living life as an undiagnosed anxious autistic person and forcing myself into situations that were overwhelming had been too much. My brain had gone, 'Nope, we can no longer function like this or endure these things without consequence. We can't cope with how we have been doing things, so now at every sign of possible stress, and at every signal with even slightly too much processing demand, we are going into panic mode.'

Perhaps my brain thought that letting everyone (and I mean literally *everyone* – even the postman) around me see my struggles would be helpful. I certainly couldn't hide them anymore.

Some people were helpful. But sadly, others were not.

I am sat in a dimly lit room on a chair that makes scratching noises each time I move. The room smells of mouldy Brussels sprouts. I know what these smell like because last year Mum forgot about a pot of them at the back of the fridge and by the time we found them, they were covered in grime. I don't like Brussels sprouts at the best of times (how anyone eats them without finding the layers uncomfortable in their mouth baffles me), let alone when they smelled like that.

A woman wearing a black cardigan with a stethoscope around her neck sits in front of the computer, tapping on the keyboard with her pristine nails. Red, the colour of wine. Every so often she turns slightly to look at me, her chair swivelling as she does so. The plastic chair I am sat in does not swivel, though I wish it did. Spinning around from side to side feels nice.

I feel agitated. I know that I feel agitated because my leg is bouncing up and down and I am struggling to sit still. I tap my hand restlessly on my knee, the denim of my jeans rubbing against my thumb.

'What do you find hard about experiencing panic attacks?' she asks, peering at me over her glasses, shaped like cats' eyes. They are objectively too large for her face, the matte bronze rim threatening to slide off the bridge of her nose.

'Having panic attacks,' I reply, finding the question absurd. What does she think could possibly be hard about losing control and struggling to breathe at any given moment of the day?

'I need you to work with me, Emily,' she sighs condescendingly, pushing her spectacles back up her nose with her forefinger.

'I am!' I raise my voice slightly, indignantly. I don't like the way that she talks to me. And I don't understand what she means. I am answering her questions. They just aren't good questions.

'She's finding this quite hard, because the appointment was meant to be 40 minutes ago, and she's late to meet her friends, and she struggles with being late,' Mum explains, placing her hand on my knee to stop it from bouncing. This aggravates me more.

'Unfortunately, I cannot control how much appointments overrun,' the woman replies, barely glancing up from the computer screen to meet Mum's gaze.

I want to tell her that is ridiculous. A sign hangs from the wall behind her, paint peeling off at the edges. The words are typed in a big font: 'Appointments limited to five minutes. Apologies for any inconveniences.' I catch Mum staring at it too. Neither of us say anything, too stumped by the woman's attitude.

'So, you're telling me that you're still having panic attacks?'

I nod, without speaking. A lump has formed in my throat. Maybe I'm having an allergic reaction. I consider telling her this, since she is a doctor, but I decide against it. I don't like her very much. I would rather have the allergic reaction.

'Have you been doing those breathing exercises the other doctor gave you a few months ago?'

Oh yes. A previous doctor had printed out a sheet from the computer. He'd passed it to me, the ink still warm, and told me that following the exercises would help to reduce my panic attacks. I had nodded earnestly, willing to try anything that might help. But when I got home and looked at the sheet, all it said was to breathe in and out three times, twice a day. That was the supposed solution.

'Yes,' I sniffle.

'If you were doing those breathing exercises, you wouldn't still be having panic attacks.'

Normally, I am quite subdued in front of strangers, but this angers me. 'Are you saying that I'm lying?'

She shrugs, seemingly unbothered. I feel my breathing quicken and a sob rise in my body. I can't talk to her. I stand up shakily. My knees wobble, as if made of paper.

'I'm leaving. This is ridiculous.' I reach for the doorknob, my palms clammy with sweat.

'Emily, please,' Mum begins to say, but I'm already storming out of the room. The door slams behind me. I know it is rude, and that is why I do it.

I wait outside by the door to the building. I expect Mum to follow me out immediately, but she doesn't. A car pulls up in the parking lot, a Volkswagen, sparkling clean. A man in his late fifties gets out of the driver's seat, then opens the passenger's side for a woman I presume is his wife. They walk towards me and I stand aside to let them in to the surgery. I wonder what brings them here today.

Mum appears five minutes later. She looks tired. I think the last few months have aged her. Sometimes I forget that she lost her father not so long ago. It is easy to get absorbed in my own head.

'Come on then,' she says, clicking the key to unlock the car.

'What happened?' I ask nervously, afraid she is upset at me for storming out.

'I asked her to refer you to CAMHS,' she replies.

'Oh.' CAMHS is the Child and Adolescent Mental Health Services. I heard Mum discussing this with my auntie last week.

In the car, Mum adjusts the rear-view mirror, smacking her lips together to rub in her lipstick. Then she pulls out of the car park, the sound of stones grinding underneath the tyres. As we drive away in silence, I vow that I won't ever go back to the GP again.

I am dropped off at the bowling alley to meet my friends. I am excited to see them, but the venue is loud and the lights are too bright. The noise of the coins in the arcade overpowers my ability to function and I find myself curled up in a ball, unable to breathe, surrounded by my friends and strangers. A staff member takes me and a friend into a side room, where we sit uncomfortably until Dad arrives to pick me up. Early. Again. I decide that I won't ever go back there either.

*

Panic attacks can feel so intense and frightening that the person experiencing them – regardless of whether or not they are autistic – may feel like they are dying.

They may struggle to help themselves through it, especially if they have not had many before. But there are things that people around us can do to help.

HOW TO HELP SOMEONE HAVING A PANIC ATTACK

» Stay calm. Speak slowly and calmly. The person may struggle to understand what you are saying because voices may sound further away or jumbled. This doesn't mean you should speak louder.

» Get them some water, but don't force them to drink it. Sometimes just the feel of the cup and their lips touching the cold water can be grounding.

» Offer them any practical things that they usually use to manage stress, like ear defenders, headphones, a weighted blanket, ice to squeeze or fidget toys.

» Remind them that they will get through this. They have before (assuming this is not the first time), so they will again.

» Reassure them they do not need to feel guilty or embarrassed.

» Help them to a quiet place if they can move or wait until they are able to.

» Tell them to try to focus on your voice instead of the anxiety.

» Encourage them to breathe with you: try counting slowly, inhaling for four and exhaling for four.

» Do not touch them, unless they state otherwise (some people may find touch or tight pressure like hugs grounding, but for others – particularly autistic people – touch can be very distressing).

» Ask them if they want to hold onto your hand, as this can be grounding.
» Ask them to place their feet firmly on the ground and focus on feeling the ground beneath their feet. Don't force them if they can't.
» Try to help them to cool down, as they may be overheating and sweating. Open a window or door for fresh air. Give them an ice cube to squeeze.
» When they are aware of their surroundings, ask them for five things they can see, four things they can hear, three things they can feel, two things they can smell and one thing they can taste.
» Don't worry if they don't respond to you at first. It doesn't mean you are doing anything wrong. Anxiety can be very overwhelming and it can take time to come out of a panic attack.
» Ask them what would help if it happened again.

Ultimately, what helps someone experiencing a panic attack varies from person to person. If you know someone who experiences them, it is best to always ask *them* what helps. If they are not sure, you may be able to support them to find out through trial and error.

Professional support may be needed if panic attacks are a regular occurrence. But, as you can see from my experience, this is not always easy to access. Especially for autistic people, who may find it difficult to communicate their needs or identify their emotions. And perhaps even more so for those undiagnosed, who can't explain why this is hard.

One of the reasons this is so challenging for many autistic people is alexithymia. Translating from the Greek to 'no words for emotion', alexithymia describes a person's inability to identify and describe the emotions they are experiencing.

Although alexithymia occurs among non-autistic people too, it is much more common among autistic people, with some research studies suggesting it affects 50 per cent of us, compared to 5 per cent of non-autistic people.[6] While I can recognise that I am feeling a negative emotion, it can be hard to identify what negative emotion that is. And sometimes I can't tell the difference between anxiety and excitement because they produce similar bodily sensations. It wasn't really until this point in my life, when I was required to talk about my emotions on a deeper level, that this became apparent. I didn't know why I was having panic attacks. I couldn't identify when I was on the verge of having one. I couldn't explain how I was feeling to others.

Through all of this, I began to feel very alone.

CHAPTER SEVEN

'Throughout it all, you are still, always, you:
beautiful and bruised, known and unknowable.'
—Leila Sales, 'This Song Will Save Your Life'

It is a sunny day in late September. It doesn't quite feel like summer is over, and autumn hasn't yet shown its face. The trees still hold tightly onto their leaves, a deep shade of green. They are home to birds that haven't yet migrated for the winter.

A small, dove-like bird hops from branch to branch in front of me. Its body is coloured in a beautiful orange and brown pattern, contrasted by its pink neck and white belly. Its tail flops proudly out behind it as it hops, its white tip illuminated by the sunlight. It is seeking every last moment of rest before its long journey to somewhere warmer. I envy it. I wish I could go somewhere safer, somewhere less dark and cold.

I am sitting on a picnic blanket, surrounded by three of my four best friends. So far, secondary school has been an easy ride in terms of friendships. The five of us have been good friends since Year 7. Since day one, when we all clocked each other and thought, *Yes, they look like decent people.* We don't really argue – in fact, the only time we do is when I am being stubborn and pedantic. I don't feel judged by them. We have similar values and interests. Unlike most teenagers at school, our friendship group has never needed to be shifted.

We have just started Year 10 and we are moaning about our chemistry teacher, who spent the entirety of our second lesson telling us to copy things out of a textbook. I don't like chemistry much anyway. I have very little interest in the subject, but my high grades mean I am in set one alongside others who have *too* much interest in the subject. I find myself struggling to concentrate and have to go over the lesson content at home after each lesson. I find the practical tasks confusing – the instructions aren't clear and I struggle to follow them.

I am sprawled out on the picnic blanket. Edie, Carys and Jasmin are rummaging through the basket of food. Carys dips a raspberry in chocolate spread. Strawberry pencils hang from between Jasmin's teeth. She tugs at one to break it, swallowing the half already in her mouth. Edie lies with her face basking in the sun, her legs crossed. A ladybug crawls up her thigh and she flicks it off delicately.

'I preferred our teacher last year,' Carys says. I agree. Our Year 9 chemistry teacher was enthusiastic, kind and patient. She made me not dread a science lesson for the first time in secondary school.

I am about to verbally agree when the conversation suddenly shifts.

'Are you okay? You've been a bit quiet,' Carys asks quietly, turning to me.

'Yeah, you have actually.' Edie rolls over onto her front, her face scrunched up in concern. 'What's up?'

They know that I am having a hard time at school. The past two weeks of term have been like the end of last term. I struggle to make it into lessons, choosing instead to hide away in the library. When I do go to class, I often leave to have a panic attack. My friends take it in turns to sit by me, to calm me down and comfort me – except our teachers are now saying they can't do that, because it is disrupting their learning time. I would agree, but they are all smart enough for it to not affect their grades.

I shrug, deliberating over whether to tell them. I don't want them to worry, but I'm used to telling them everything and I feel like I need to tell someone. Not doing so is eating away at me.

'I hurt myself last night,' I stammer. My hands pick at the grass next to me, tearing it away from its roots. Then I feel guilty for killing it. So, I try to stop, but my hands are restless.

The three of them stare at me, not having expected that. I hadn't either. Carys and Jasmin exchange a worried glance, neither of them knowing what to say.

'Please don't tell anyone,' I add hastily, biting my lip. The metallic taste of blood fills my mouth. 'I just didn't know what to do.'

I had sat alone in my bedroom, my hands shaking, the idea racing around my head. The anxiety yesterday had been too much. It is always too much. I had tried to distract myself from the idea and even reached out to an online chat service, but in the end, I think I *wanted* to act on it. Afterwards, I laid on my bed, feeling the rise and fall of my chest and the ache of my leg. I felt adrenaline racing through my veins. Like a renewed sense of energy within me. In those minutes, my anxiety had dissipated and I had felt relief. Calmness.

'I feel like you should tell someone,' Edie says nervously, tucking her blonde hair behind her ear.

My eyes widen, imagining the look on my parents' faces when they inevitably found out. Would they be angry? Disappointed? Devastated? The thought of their reaction and being in trouble makes my blood rush. 'No. Please. I can't.'

Jasmin leans across the blanket and throws her arms around me. Even in a short black dress, she feels warm and my body relaxes. A wave of emotion comes over me. Tears prick at my eyelids.

'Do you want to talk about what happened?' Carys asks uncertainly.

I shake my head quickly. They don't need that. I just needed to tell them.

'Can you at least talk to one of us if you feel that way again?' Jasmin asks.

'I'll try,' I promise, knowing that will be unlikely.

Carys pops another raspberry into her mouth. I lean forward and grab one too, dipping it in the oozing chocolate Jasmin had melted at home. There is silence. None of us really know what to say. We haven't dealt with this kind of thing before. We talk about everything – periods, parents, drama – but not things like *this*. Never anything like this. The conversation soon starts up again, with Jasmin talking about a boy in her maths class, but none of us forget what has been shared.

Research into self-harm reports a variety of potential risk factors. These include things like age, gender, background, family situation and so on. However, there is another risk factor, which hits me hard, and that is autism.[1,2]

Just by being autistic, you are at a greater risk of harming yourself.

And, when you consider that 1 in 4 14-year-old girls have self-harmed,[3,4] the prognosis for autistic kids is particularly bleak.

Of course, much of this research is based on the ways that society views self-harm. We tend to see self-harm as one or two particular methods, but alcohol abuse, unprotected sex and impulsive behaviour can all be forms of self-harm. So, when they say that girls are more likely to self-harm, it may just be that girls are more likely to self-harm in the ways we deem to be self-harm, while boys do it in ways we don't yet view as such.

Self-harm is when somebody hurts themselves, usually to try to cope with difficult emotions, distressing memories or stressful situations. There are many reasons why someone might turn to it. It could be because they are feeling so much emotional pain that turning it into physical pain makes it more manageable. They may feel that it brings them a sense of control, or that it decreases the negative feelings consuming them, or that it is a way of punishing themselves for something they feel imprisoned by. They may feel dissociated or numb, and self-harming might momentarily help to bring them back into the present. They may find it hard to process emotions and find that self-harm helps to release them. The reasons are endless and are different for every single person.

We also know – and this is very important – that not everyone who self-harms is suicidal. And self-harming doesn't necessarily *lead* to someone being suicidal, though a high proportion of those who do attempt suicide have a history of self-harm.[5] I know this is important, because the day that my mum was called into my school and told that I was self-harming, she did not know what that meant.*

When she found out, we had to have a conversation of course. We didn't straight away. We went to Sainsbury's, in fact, for reasons that are still not clear to me. We browsed the aisles looking for different pasta sauces, pop-tarts and strawberry- flavoured milk, avoiding the elephant in the room that had led to us being in the supermarket when I was meant to be at school.† On the cereal aisle, I spotted my

---

* How and why this happened I will explain in the next chapter, but for now let's concentrate on self-harm.

† 'The elephant in the room' is one of my favourite idioms that makes no apparent sense, though it supposedly means to avoid talking about an obvious problem.

grandmother pottering along with a basket in her hands. Mum and I hid; she did not want to answer questions about why I was there.

I don't remember exactly when or how the topic was brought up, but it must have been eventually. We avoided it for a long time, though. Neither of us knew how to approach it; and I just wouldn't open up about it. Because how do you talk about something like self-harm?

At home, I refused to talk about it with my parents. They didn't know what to say, becoming tearful when they mentioned it, so sometimes it felt like I was treading on eggshells. I would shut down when it was mentioned, unwilling to discuss it. I was upset that they knew, the secret I had been carrying around for over a half a year no longer only mine.

I am lying on my bed, staring at the ceiling. The stipple design looks like popcorn kernels stuck underneath paint. My eyes dart between them, conjuring up shapes in my mind. Anything to try to distract myself.

The muffled whispers I have been trying to drown out suddenly quieten. The familiar click of the kitchen door opening, then closing, echoes through the hallway, the sound waves passing through the gap in my bedroom door. The light tap of footsteps climbing the stairs. Mum's. Dad's are heavier, more of a pound. My siblings' quicker, springier.

Sure enough, seconds later, Mum appears in my doorway. Her face is ever so slightly flushed, her expression unreadable. She steps into my room and leans against my desk, putting down a bowl of freshly washed strawberries.

I feel my heart rate quicken and blood rush to my head as I anticipate what she could be about to say.

'Have you got anything on at the weekend?' she asks, her voice strained.

I shake my head, returning my gaze to the ceiling, hoping she will leave. Our interactions have felt uncomfortable lately, neither of us quite knowing what to say. I feel on edge, constantly uncertain of when or if she will mention it again.

'Maybe we can go shopping?' she suggests.

I shrug. 'Okay.'

She lingers for a moment, quiet. I don't look at her.

'Dinner is in an hour.'

I nod, turning as she leaves, gently closing my door behind her. The strawberries sit on my desk. I don't particularly have an appetite, but I reach for them anyway. My whole body feels restless. This is not unusual, but the feeling has heightened in the weeks following the Sainsbury's day.

For so long, this has been my secret. Sure, I told Edie, Carys, and Jasmin eight months ago when it first happened. And I have reached out to Edie a few times since. But that has always been on my terms; and them knowing is different. They don't really know the extent of it. How I will spend much of the day at school thinking about coming home and hurting myself. How every time something goes wrong, or when I think that something could, I reassure myself with the promise of punishing myself that evening.

Just being able to think about it makes me feel powerful, like I have a solution for when bad things happen. A means of distracting myself. Of feeling something – surely *anything* must be better than being stuck in these cycles in my mind. Sometimes it makes me feel lighter, freer. Other times, heavier. But that heaviness is more enticing than the heaviness of the thoughts that entrap me. Because I have control over this one.

Now my secret is no longer mine. Mum and Dad know. School know. Goodness knows who else knows. I had to talk to my teacher. My head is beginning to explode. The thoughts, or that voice in my head that isn't me, has been getting too loud. I need that to stop. But I still feel angry, that now *this* is no longer just mine. Mum and Dad are looking at me differently. They want me to talk about it, I think. But I can't. My throat is clogged up. They don't understand. Nobody does.

My phone buzzes next to me. A text from Edie, checking in after I shut myself in the toilet at lunchtime to cry.

Hope you're ok. Why don't you open one of your letters?

I pull at the chipped blue knob on my desk drawer and grab the stack of letters. Sixteen envelopes high, each one bordered with silver, pink or blue glitter around a sentence. I discard the top two, already opened in the week since I was given them. I skim the remaining ones, searching for one that resonates. My eyes land on the bottom envelope. Edie's writing in large cursive letters – 'Open when you feel lonely'.

I slide my fingers under the seal and pull out the orange card inside, careful not to rip the paper. This is the first one of Edie's I've read; the others were Jasmin's and Carys's. My eyes scan the page.

When you feel lonely . . . There shouldn't be a need for you to be reading this card because you are never alone, and you never will be. So many people love you and care about you beyond your imagination. Not a day goes by where there isn't somebody thinking of you, so however down and alone you currently feel, remember all of your friends and family however distant love you with all their hearts. Love from E xx

I feel tears well up in my eyes and blink rapidly to force them away. I'm not quite sure how I got so lucky to have them as my friends. They now know that my secret is out, that school and my parents know what's been going on. I didn't tell them at first. I had tried to blame my period as the reason for my heightened emotions, but they had seen right through me. So, I had told them. And a week later, they had presented me with a wooden basket, filled with envelopes containing these letters. Each one has a different instruction: 'Open when you need a laugh', 'Open on a bad day', 'Open when you feel anxious' and so on.

I have the best friends.

I do not deserve them.

It had never been a cry for help, but I suppose a very small part of me was relieved that other people knew how bad I felt.

HOW TO TALK TO SOMEONE ABOUT SELF-HARM (IF YOU ARE THE ONE SELF-HARMING)

» Be kind to yourself and remind yourself how brave you are.
» Ask someone you trust if you can talk to them – that could be a parent, an older sibling, an aunt, a teacher or a friend. Or, if that is too difficult, write them a letter.
» You don't have to tell them; you could show them.
» Remember you can take breaks during the conversation.
» If they get upset, try to reassure yourself that they are not upset with you. They are most likely upset that you feel this way.
» Sit with the silence – it can feel uncomfortable, but it can be meaningful.

HOW TO TALK TO SOMEONE YOU LOVE ABOUT SELF-HARM (IF THEY ARE THE ONE SELF-HARMING)

» Research self-harm. Go into the conversation with understanding.
» Try starting a conversation while doing something together such as baking or dog-walking. Formal conversations can be harder.
» Don't put too much pressure on one conversation. You can go back to it later.
» Tell them that you're not angry, disappointed or upset with them. Avoid making them feel guilty.
» Offer to help clean or dress the wound, but don't force them.
» Tell them that they can always reach out to you if they feel the need to self-harm.
» Offer to create an alert system so they don't have to explicitly tell you if that is too hard. Perhaps they can text you a code word or put a sad face on their bedroom door.
» Try to make it feel 'normal' to talk about. This can make it easier.
» Talk to someone you trust too for support if you need it.
» Talk through possible triggers.
» If they won't talk to you, it might just be that they're not ready. Give them some time and space if it is safe to do so.

Despite my initial reticence, talking about it got easier with time. Eventually my parents and I didn't have a choice but to talk about it. But it would have been easier if we had implemented some of these strategies from the beginning.

For the people doing it, self-harming can feel like the

loneliest place in the world. I didn't know when I started that it would later become an addiction. Something I had to do to be able to function. Something I couldn't go two minutes without thinking about. Something that would nearly kill me.

It can feel like nobody understands. But that isn't true. Here is a letter, for those of you struggling with self-harm, or those of you who have in the past.

Dear you,

I want you to know that you are loved, valued and cared for. You may feel invisible, but I see you right this minute. You may feel that hurting yourself is the only way to manage right now, and I understand that feeling. I know how it feels to believe that self-harming is the only way to get through the day; so, for this moment, I am not going to invalidate that. But I want you to know that you are beautiful, unique and treasured. No matter what you are blaming yourself for, you deserve peace. You have gone through enough hell already.

Talking helps. It can be so hard, especially at first and especially if self-harm has been your secret for a long time. Letting go of that control and feeling like you are potentially risking your only coping mechanism can feel impossible. It can be as much of an addiction as an alcohol or drug addiction. It isn't your fault.

But self-harm doesn't have to be your only coping mechanism.

Over the years I have sat in hundreds of appointments with mental health professionals and had dozens of conversations with my teachers where I was told that I didn't have to self-harm. But – and I'm sorry if you know this too – it didn't feel that way. I genuinely felt compelled to self-harm, and I believed it to be the only way I could manage my distress and my emotions.

So, I do know that people telling you that 'there are other ways to cope' can feel invalidating and insensitive. And at times it may be the only way you can survive; and you are incredible for surviving. But I am going to tell you some ways anyway. Because maybe you want them. And maybe, just maybe, one day one of them will work. And I don't want you to keep hurting yourself.

WHAT YOU COULD DO INSTEAD OF SELF-HARMING*

» Squeeze an ice cube.
» Have a cold shower or a hot bath.
» Go for a run or a walk.
» Call a crisis line such as the Samaritans.
» Reread encouraging texts or letters.
» Hug a family member or a pet.
» Cry.
» Write in a journal.
» Watch a horror film as a distraction.
» Tear paper apart.
» Clap your hands until they sting.
» Break something.
» Observe the thought and sit with the thought, not judging yourself for it.
» Doodle.
» Watch a funny video.

---

* I know that none of these things provide a substitute for the way that self-harm appears to help you. But sometimes it is about getting through that moment by doing anything else you possibly can.

» Hit a pillow or a punchbag.
» Call a friend and talk to them.
» Do henna on your arms.

And, because I care about you (and if you want to read them), here are some reasons why you should not self-harm if you are feeling the need to:

» Nobody deserves to be hurt.
» You wouldn't tell your friend, or your younger self, to self-harm, and you deserve the same love that you give to other people.
» There are safer ways to find relief from the pain you are feeling inside, and you deserve to find those ways.
» The relief from hurting yourself doesn't last; it doesn't solve the problem; the urge will only return.
» Your body isn't to blame for anything; your body loves you and will do everything it can to repair itself afterwards.
» Self-harming reinforces the bad things that others have said to you, and those things aren't true.
» You are not to blame for anything that has happened to you.
» The pain for weeks afterwards and the effort of having to cover and hide the scars aren't worth it.
» You don't deserve the pain.
» One day you will see yourself for the absolute joy and beauty that you are. Hold on for that moment.

All my love, your friend, Emily

CHAPTER EIGHT

'Torture: knowing something makes no sense,
but doing it anyway.'
—Corey Ann Haydu

When I was ten, I got head lice. Yes, those delightful creepy-crawlies that suck blood from your scalp to live and lay dozens of nits that then hatch into more lice. Sorry if I've got you scratching already.

My hairdresser found them, which was a lovely experience and massively helped with my hatred of hairdressers. I had never felt such disgust at myself before. Although – fun fact – head lice actually prefer clean hair, I felt dirty. I wanted to rip all of my hair and my skin off.

Obviously, my mum got rid of the lice, with that awful-smelling solution most parents have to buy from the chemist at some point in their child's life. We sat in the bath for a very uncomfortable hour or two while she scraped them all out. My legs came up in rashes from the bath water, my head hurt from the comb and my nose was sore from the stench. But I sat patiently because I wanted to not feel disgusting anymore.

When I got out of the bath, dried my hair and got into my pyjamas, the relief I felt was indescribable. The difference between feeling disgusting to feeling clean was of a magnitude I hadn't experienced before. The relief was all-encompassing.

I had thought it was over and that I would never need to feel that sheer repulsion and anxiety again. But, the following week, a thought crept into my head. *Your head itched just then, didn't it? I think you have nits again.*

I told Mum. She scraped through my hair with the nit comb and concluded there was nothing there. But I couldn't believe her. She had missed them before; surely she was missing them again. And perhaps there was only one or two there this time, because I caught it early. I had seen the kid I sat next to in class scratch their head once that day and I couldn't let that go.

So, off Mum went back to the chemist that evening to buy another bottle of head-lice solution. Again, we sat in the bath and she drenched my hair in the oily liquid. I imagined the head lice festering in my hair being destroyed. But Mum didn't find any on her comb. I didn't have nits. The fact that I had endured the process again for no reason didn't bother me, though. The relief rushed over me once again, because this time I was sure that I was clean – that everything was okay. I went to bed on a high, vowing to keep my hair up at school and to avoid going too close to any of my classmates.

Unfortunately, a week later my guard dropped, because there is only so long a ten-year-old can constantly remind themselves not to go too near to other people before something distracts them and they forget. And it wasn't even that I *did* go too close to someone. I probably hadn't. It was the fact that for five minutes or so I had forgotten to *think* about the distance of my head from other people's. My brain said, *Your heads could have touched and you wouldn't have known. And didn't you see that boy scratch his head yesterday?*

So, for a third time, Mum went to the pharmacy to buy the solution to kill the non-existent buggers. I was embarrassed just thinking of what the pharmacist must have thought about me. But, once again, there were none. This time I vowed not to bother Mum with it again, understanding that I was convincing myself of something that wasn't there.

Except, every time that I itched my hair, I thought I had lice. I imagined them living on my head, sucking my blood, clustering in swarms, and I felt dirty and disgusting. Some days it was all I could think about. I felt physically low and didn't enjoy the activities I was doing. So, I took it upon myself to get rid of them on my own, just in case they were there. Every day before my shower, I combed through my hair with the nit comb Mum had kept from the treatments. I peered in the mirror as I did so, looking closely at my scalp. I convinced myself that any small speck of dust I saw was an egg, feeling the anxiety settle in as soon as I spotted it. When Mum and Dad went out, I put conditioner through my hair as if it were the treatment. I stood in front of the mirror and brushed through my hair with the comb and kitchen towel, just like my mum had done. This sometimes bought me relief but more often didn't, because I could have missed a spot. It was these could-haves that consumed me.

Doing all of this and worrying about it took up a lot of time. It continued for years. And it always got worse when I knew the hairdresser's was coming up, even though I avoided them as much as I possibly could.

I still hate the hairdresser's, even now.

WHY I HATE THE HAIRDRESSER'S

» I hate people touching my hair.
» The pain of them tugging at my hair.
» The small talk.
» The sound of the scissors ('snip-snip-snip'). The feeling of cut hair on my back.
» My hair has to get wet.
» Having to stare at myself in a mirror during the haircut.
» The fact that a lot more of my hair is always cut off than we had agreed at the start.

» How many people's hair has been cut with these scissors?
» There is always hair everywhere.
» The loud music they play in the salon is irritating.
» Having to sit still is impossible.
» Not only having to sit still, but exactly evenly so your hair doesn't get cut wonkily.
» There is a lot of time to think.
» The strong smells of the products.
» There is always a crying child.
» They found nits in my hair.

It is only in recent years that I recognise the pattern that I went through for what it was. The obsession and compulsion cycle of Obsessive-Compulsive Disorder (OCD). The obsession being that I had head lice, and the compulsion being that I needed to check this and then get rid of them.

The thing with OCD is that it morphs from topic to topic over time. Not only that, but it is sneaky. When I was 13, it convinced me that it was my friend. That it would help me overcome my anxiety. And I listened to it.

Touch each book on your bookcase ten times and you won't have a panic attack today.

This thought that has just popped into my head is strange. It doesn't feel like my thought. Except it must be because it is inside my head.

I ponder over it for a while. I know that logically the thought doesn't make sense. But I also know that if I don't listen to it, I will definitely have a panic attack – and perhaps if I do listen, there is a small chance that I won't.

I must stop having panic attacks. The geography GCSE trip to Italy is coming up. I have been looking forward to it for over a year. My four best friends are all going. One of the geography teachers has already suggested to Mum and Dad that it might be better if I don't go. I imagine the history teachers have had a word with them. Mum and Dad were furious at the suggestion, saying that they can't discriminate against me for a health condition and arguing that they need to put in place reasonable adjustments. Soon there is going to be a big meeting. I know that my panic attacks need to reduce and be less severe for me to be able to go. I need my anxiety to stop taking over.

Pulling my school jumper over my head and flattening down my hair, I move towards my bookcase. It stands tall and proud in the corner of my room, a pretty impressive show of books for someone of my age. It is filled with a mixture of my favourites: classics like *Wuthering Heights* and *Jane Eyre*, teenage rom-coms like *The Life of Riley*, spy novels like the *Alex Rider* books, series like *Divergent* and *Twilight*, and of course huge collections from Enid Blyton. I love being whisked away on the Wishing-Chair or up the Faraway Tree. Her adventures are neverending.

I take a deep breath, filling my lungs with air. Feeling silly, I lift up my finger. I drift it softly along each book, tapping each one ten times. I count out loud. *One. Two. Three. Four. Five. Six. Seven. Eight. Nine. Ten.* Then onto the next one. At first the books feel soft under my touch, but the more I tap, the rougher they feel from the friction.

I am on the bottom row when Mum's shrill voice sounds up the stairs. 'Emily! We're late!'

I glance at my phone. It is 8.15. We usually leave for school at 8.10. Panic rises in my chest. I'm not done. I can't leave yet. I stare at *The Secret Garden*, the book my finger is hovering over. My mind has gone blank. I realise that I can't remember how many times I have tapped it. I begin to count again from one, but it doesn't feel right. I need to get it right. I move back to the start of the row and try again.

By the time I am done and plonk myself in the car, Mum is angry with me. But, for the first time since my panic attacks began, a blanket of calmness drapes me on the way to school. I flick through the WhatsApp messages from my friends. Carys says she is sick today and won't be coming in. I tap back a message wishing her well. I am about to press send when the tyres screech to a halt and I am thrusted forward in my seat. The seatbelt scrapes against my neck, leaving a mark.

'Mummm,' Thomas moans, slamming his pen down on his exercise book. There is a pen mark scrawled across the page, the jolt having taken him by surprise.

'Serves you right for doing your homework now,' I tut, like the irritating older sister that I am. I always do my homework on the day that I get it.

'Don't be so mean,' he mutters, turning to face out the window. I do the same. The cars speed past us, exceeding the speed limit magnificently. I hope we don't have a car accident. We could have had one then, couldn't we? Mum could crash on her way home. Anything could happen. A piece of garbage in the road, a gust of wind knocking her concentration.

Tap the window three times and Mum will be safe all day.

I feel my fingers against the window, damp from the condensation. My anxiety dissipates. I feel a sense of power. Like maybe this way I can control my anxiety. Almost like magic.

My obedience to these thoughts gets me to Italy.

Before I know it, I am on Italian soil for the first time, soaking up the sunshine. I am standing on dry rocks – large rocks, the sort that it would take heavy machinery to move. The view of the rocks fading out to sea is a type of beautiful that I have never seen before. My eyes linger on the sea – a clear blue, nothing like the green murky water that they call sea in Devon. Here you can see right through it, like glass, to the rocks and the fish that swim below. Eyes to a whole habitat beneath the sea's surface. The ripples through the water are so delicate that they don't even seem like waves.

Further out, there are the outlines of mountains scattering the horizon. The blue of the sky almost melts into them. The mountains look blue from here too. It's a picture of serenity. Just looking at the scene fills my body with calmness.

Next to my feet are small pools of water bordering the rocks, where fish the size of buttons dance around together. I kneel beside them, in awe at the way their tiny bodies wriggle and jump. They take shelter in clusters of white and orange corals, positioned to provide shade from the hot sun. I too would like to move to shade.

I stand back up and look over to where the others are sitting on the rocks, dipping their toes in the sparkling water. I can imagine this must be cooling, but I know that I will hate the feeling of wet feet that I can't dry properly and that they will rub against my shoes, blistering them. I would rather stay dry.

Edie notices me staring and calls out. 'You find anything?'

'Just fish. They seem happy,' I grin, wandering over to them and taking a seat beside her and Jasmin. Edie's honey-coloured hair wraps around her shoulders in waves, kept off her face by the sunglasses perching on her head.

'How long do we have left?' Carys asks, appearing from behind a rock. She is holding a clump of seaweed and tosses it back into the water. It creates a small splash, but almost instantaneously the stillness returns.

Edie, knowing the question is directed at her, looks at her watch. She is the only one who wears one, and it is very useful for the rest of us. Our phones are all off to save battery. 'Ten minutes.'

I inhale deeply, allowing the sea air to flood my lungs. I close my eyes briefly, wanting to soak in every minute of this before we have to cram back onto the hot coach.

'Shall we get an ice cream then?' Carys suggests, already on her feet.

We nod and stand up. Edie and Jasmin shake their feet, droplets spraying to the ground, and slide them back into their shoes. I am glad my feet are dry.

We walk across the rocks, our backs now to the sea. There is a small ice cream shop just across the road from the beach. The sort that looks like a family-owned business. The road is quiet; barely a car has passed in the time we have been on the rocks. Still, we look both ways before crossing. And there I catch sight of him.

A man, in his late forties, with a dishevelled beard slightly covered by a newspaper, peers out from behind a postbox. He has large dark sunglasses on and a blue cap pulled right over his forehead. Strands of sweaty dark hair fall out of the sides. He is less than ten metres away – and has been the entire time.

He has followed us everywhere. In the hotel, through Sorrento, across the ruins at Pompeii, up Mount Vesuvius – a volcano I was sure was about to explode as we climbed it – and now, along the Amalfi Coast. His car is parked up nearby, an old Fiat 500 that should have been taken off the road years ago. It is far too small for him; he barely fits behind the wheel.

'Oop, there he is!' Jasmin giggles, following my gaze. It is like a game of Where's Wally, everywhere we go.

'Do you think your dad would like an ice cream?' Carys asks. She's being sincere, but I shoot a glare of frustration at her. Then I hush her. There is a group of girls from our year not too far away, licking ice creams they must have just bought.

'Oh, they can't hear us. They would think they had misheard anyway!'

I am desperate for no one else to find out that the only way I was allowed to come on the school trip to Italy was for my dad to be no more than ten metres away from me at all times. This was the result of a risk assessment drawn up by a teacher who barely knew me and had labelled every part of the itinerary as a 'definite' panic attack. My parents were furious. According to their assessment, I was due to have had 20 panic attacks a day at least. I am behind schedule.

Apart from my friends, who would recognise the man following us, the other kids have walked past him repeatedly, sat behind him on the plane and shared a hotel with him, and have no idea that he is my father. Or indeed that a 48-year-old man has been stalking us. And that is the way it will stay for the whole trip.

'Honeycomb, please,' I say to the shopkeeper as I reach the front of the queue. Honeycomb is the closest flavour to hokey pokey, a New Zealand special, and it is my favourite.

I watch the lady wash her hands before she dispenses it. She hurriedly slaps the soap onto her hands, missing her thumb. She uses the thumb to touch my cone. I deliberate over whether I should eat it or not and decide it will be okay if I wipe three squirts of hand gel over my hands first and then throw away the part of the cone that her thumb touched. I don't want to get ill.

'Em, your hands won't stop bleeding if you use that much hand gel.' Jasmin taps my cracked hand gently, encouraging me to shut the bottle. They are sore, but I have only done two squirts. When she turns to order her ice cream, strawberry flavoured as always, I squirt on a third.

*

This was the start of OCD sneaking into my life properly and tricking me into believing that it was my friend. It told me that if I did certain things then the anxieties that had been ruling my head for the past year wouldn't come true.

Sometimes, it sounded like this:

Anxiety: If you go to the cinema, you will have a panic attack.
OCD: If you tap the desk ten times, you won't have a panic attack.

And sometimes, it sounded like this:

Anxiety: Your mum will die in a car crash today.
OCD: Tap all your books ten times, then again ten times, then again, then again . . . and she won't have a car crash.

I listened, and it helped.

For a while, this wasn't too much of a problem. I was thankful that I had found a way to control my anxiety. The visible signs of my anxiety reduced. My panic attacks got less frequent. I felt comfortable that OCD (although I didn't have a name for it then) would keep me safe.

But, after Italy, my fears of contamination became all-consuming and people around me began to notice. My hands bled constantly from washing them too much, and they hurt. A lot. It felt like they were burning and they would bleed all over my work. I remember my history teacher giving me a tissue in class because blood was staining my exercise book as I wrote. I started being late for class because I made sure that I washed my hands between lessons, and many, many more times throughout the day than normal people do. I completed rituals to ensure my family wouldn't get ill.

The worries were beginning to consume my brain.

One, two, three, I count, as my hand taps the lamp post. My chapped hands are cloaked immediately with dust, clinging to the dry blood stuck to my skin. I don't brush it off; it blocks the cuts from leaking. I pump hand gel three times onto them and brace myself for the sting.

I walk five steps to the next lamp post and tap again. *One, two, three.* Then I squirt the hand gel.

I am walking around the village that I live in, a small community built around elegant oak trees. I have lived here my entire life, moving only once, when I was five years old, to the other side of the village. I was sad about leaving Alice, but the rush of excitement moving brought was new; the exhilaration of seeing my new bedroom for the first time and the pride of being able to select the shade of baby-pink paint to cover my walls. It was a novelty that felt within my control.

It is a Sunday afternoon and I have been out the house for two hours. Mum and Dad are chaperoning Thomas and Jessica to different places. I told them I was going for a walk, but I didn't say how long I would be. And it is taking longer than I had expected. I need to touch all of the lamp posts, three times, to make sure that I don't get ill this week. It's not that I'm so fussed about being ill myself, but that I don't want to make my family ill.

I am very aware of the fact that I look stupid. I am embarrassed, so I haven't told anyone what I am doing. I keep my eyes peeled for people. When dog-walkers pass, I pretend to be staring at something on my phone. When cars drive by,

I pretend to be leaning on the lamp post to tie my shoelaces. I anxiously wait for them to pass so that I can carry on.

I figure that if I don't do this to at least *try* to keep my family safe, then I am selfish for not trying. I should try even if it doesn't work, because I am not selfish and I should care.

I would rather be at home, watching *Pretty Little Liars* – my latest obsession. I am hooked. I rewatch episode after episode, hiding away in my room for hours and googling all of the storylines. I even copy the show and set up my own SOS message with Carys, Jasmin and Edie. I know none of them will ever use it. They don't get excited about things the way that I do.

I come to the end of the road. The smell from the fish and chip shop opposite wafts up my nose, making my stomach churn. I don't know how many more roads I need to do. I can't predict what the thoughts will say. But I am desperate to go home. I need a wee and I just want to curl up in bed.

You didn't do it properly. You need to do this road again.

I stare back down the long road I just did. It must have 20 lamp posts on it at least. I feel tears prick at my eyes. One falls down my cheek. It is not gentle, but hot, angry.

'No!' I say out loud, as if arguing with myself. 'Please, no.'

I know the thoughts are mine, even though they don't feel like they are. So why can't I control them? Why do they have such a grip on me?

Tap each lamp post three times again. Or you will get ill and your family will die.

Reluctantly, I turn around and make my way back up the road. I think I need to tell someone. I don't want to be like this anymore.

*

Could my brain *realllyyy* not come up with something a little more *normal* than lamp posts? And could I *realllyyy* not have waited until *after* tapping all of the lamp posts to hand gel my hands? Because ouch, it hurt.

But I wasn't in control. OCD was in control of me. It dictated everything that I did. At this stage in my life, it consumed 99 per cent of my waking thoughts. It was in charge of what I could and couldn't do and I had surrendered myself mercilessly to it.

And, at the same time as it became all-consuming, it also grew darker. It was a voice in my head telling me that I needed to hurt myself to stop bad things happening to people I cared about. I began experiencing thoughts of hurting other people and I had to carry out certain rituals to make sure that I didn't.

This is a type of OCD called Harm OCD, where people become very distressed by thoughts of hurting others or causing harm. These thoughts do not make them dangerous or harmful – in fact, they go to extreme lengths to *not* act on the thoughts because they are so distressed and worried by them.

But the logic is deeply flawed, because violent people do not spend hours worrying about their thoughts and worrying that they are awful people. They just act on the thoughts, hurt people and take pleasure in doing so. OCD thoughts are egodystonic, meaning that they do not line up with the person's morals or values and so are very distressing to them.

Most people experience strange thoughts at some point in their life. For example, the passing thoughts of 'I could push this person right now' or 'I could hurt someone with this knife' are actually very common. Most people without OCD or anxiety are able to shake them off. They just think, 'That's a weird thought', forget about it and move on with their day. People with OCD can't do that.

According to statistics, autistic people are more likely to

suffer from OCD. Some research shows that 17 per cent of us have an OCD diagnosis,[1] compared to approximately 1.2 per cent of non-autistic people.[2]

Autistic hyperfixations or special interests can be mistaken for obsessions. Although these can be very intense and interfere with daily life, they are usually something we enjoy, which provides a sense of comfort or safety and can help us to feel more able to manage. Although going through life believing I was living in Hogwarts did not *always* help me to manage better. Not least because my school wasn't very similar to Hogwarts.

Obsessions, however, are repetitive and intrusive thoughts that cause significant distress and directly lead to compulsions to reduce the anxiety caused by that thought. Many of the most common compulsions, like ordering, needing symmetry or exactness and repeating actions, are frequently seen among autistic people but simply because these actions *help* them; they are not necessarily OCD-related compulsions. Autistic people carrying out ritualistic behaviours tend to do so quite contently. Routines are often a source of comfort. We may enjoy them, and they might help us to organise our thoughts and process what is going on around us. Our distress comes when we are prevented from carrying out our routines.

Imagine if the world was extremely overwhelming, if your brain didn't seem compatible with your surroundings and if everything that happened around you made little sense. You would want to do anything you could to make it easier for you to navigate, wouldn't you? Doing things a certain way, having a routine and maintaining order and exactness can provide a reassurance like no other. Engaging in repetitive behaviours can reduce anxiety, comfort us and make us feel good.

Although autistic traits *can* be incorrectly pathologised as

OCD symptoms, however, there is still a higher proportion of autistic people who do also have OCD. Maybe our neurodivergent brains are just wired that way. Or, maybe our autistic inability to let things go or to fixate on things makes it harder for the thoughts to just pass.

For whatever reason, we latch onto the intrusive thoughts, and they stick, like superglue. It takes a lot of work, therapy, medication, tears and exhaustion to learn how to fight them.

But all of that begins with telling someone and asking for help.

Today is Monday. The day after lamp post day. I am standing outside the pastoral support teacher's office. Miss B. I have grown to trust her over the past year, and I like her. She always smells lovely, with her signature perfume always noticeable but not so strong that I can't breathe. Her mannerisms are kind and gentle. But she is always malting. Loose strands of her dirty-blonde hair hang down her clothes and her chair. This doesn't appease me greatly, since any hair not attached to a head makes me feel queasy.

I linger in the corridor, overlooking the school hall. The chairs are all lined up, after assembly. I haven't been to an assembly in over a year. I hide away in the library instead, either chatting to the librarian or with my head in a book. Sometimes I look out of the window that overlooks the hall and watch as the PowerPoint flicks from slide to slide.

I hear noise inside Miss B's office. Someone is with her. They are talking in hushed voices. I hesitate, briefly debating whether I should leave and return to class. But I can't. I hold my shaking hand to the door and knock. The whispers pause. I am not normally nervous to talk to Miss B, but I know that I am going to open a can of worms today. That's a saying that

I learned last year. I think it means that I know I am going to cause a problem.

Her familiar voice invites me in. She is sat on her office chair, a long black dress draped over her legs. Our eyes lock straight away. Hers are sea-blue, like mine, with a strange look in them – perhaps puzzlement. The lady sitting next to her is from the curriculum-support team. She works with the boys in our class sometimes.

'I . . . I need to talk to you,' I begin, tears already starting to pour down my face. I twist the beaded bracelet that never leaves my wrist. The beads are losing their colour.

The other lady gets up, saying something about popping in later, and leaves the room. I hear her heels clicking against the floor of the corridor, growing fainter and fainter as she gets further away.

'What's wrong?' Miss B asks, concern in her voice. She ushers me into the heart of her office, closing the door behind me. I perch on the edge of the seat next to her.

I have practised what I am going to say, in front of my mirror, over and over again, but now, staring at her face, my mind goes blank. Tears stream down my cheeks, burning my skin.

'I think I need help. I can't do this anymore,' I croak.

'I might need you to explain a bit more of what you mean,' she says gently, placing a supportive hand on my knee.

The words flood back into my mind as I launch into an explanation, barely pausing for a breath. I don't even know if she can make out what I am saying between my sobs and short breaths.

'Look at my notebook.' I reach into my bag and pull out a soft brown book, a robin sewn out of pink beads on the front.

She opens the first page, then flicks to the next, then the

next. Her eyes appear slightly wider than normal as she tries to soak in the content. I have listed every single illness I could find and research, with information about symptoms, causes and preventative measures.

'I've been hurting myself as well,' I add hastily.

I don't expect her to look up so fast, but she does.

'Oh Emily,' she says softly. She gets out of her chair and walks to the blinds, pulling them down to block out the passers-by. 'Can you show me?'

I take off my tights, shame flooding me. She looks at my legs briefly, then tells me to put my tights back on and stares back down at my book.

Words gush out of my mouth now as I try to explain. But they are soon drowned out by more sobs. She swivels her chair to face me, her hands resting on her crossed knees.

'Emily. This isn't just anxiety. This sounds more like OCD. We're going to get you help.'

'O . . . OCD . . .' I stammer. I have heard of it. It's when people wash their hands a lot, I think. And I do, I suppose.

She takes a deep breath, and I know what is coming. 'But I'm going to need to tell someone. I can't keep this to myself.'

I hang my head. I knew she would have to. I don't want Mum and Dad to know, but I'm desperate. I can't keep going on like this.

Miss B leaves the room for what feels like ages. When she returns, the assistant headteacher is with her. She looks me up and down sympathetically. She tells me she has to phone my mum. I don't protest, but I don't want to be there when she tells her.

Mum is at school within 15 minutes, her work left half open on the kitchen table. Miss B takes her into a side room, and they are there for a while. I watch them through the glass.

Mum begins to cry, her head in her hands. It's when she comes out of the meeting that we drive to Sainsbury's.

That was the day I learned that there was a name for what I was experiencing. Just knowing it was OCD was a huge relief. There was a name for it. I wasn't alone. So I started to learn what OCD meant for me.

WHAT OCD IS (TO ME)

» OCD is not a quirk, a personality trait, or something that is 'cute' to have.
» OCD is not just liking things tidy, or liking things done a certain way.
» OCD is believing that you are evil, because of the bad thoughts you have.
» OCD is crying at 3am because the horrific images of you hurting someone won't go away.
» OCD is believing that everything you do could cause someone you care about to die.
» OCD is redoing a piece of writing three times, because if you don't something bad will happen.
» OCD is spending hours tapping an object until it feels like you have done it just enough times for everyone to be okay.
» OCD is constantly running late because the compulsions you did were never quite enough.
» OCD is your raw hands burning from washing them too many times.
» OCD is feeling like you are drowning in your own mind.

» OCD is praying for two hours before you go to bed, even if you're not sure if you believe in God, because if you don't then you might go to Hell and burn in flames forever.
» OCD is constantly feeling guilty for not doing enough to stop your family being hurt.
» OCD is feeling like you are going to make everyone around you ill.
» OCD promises you that it will keep you safe. It slips into your life quietly, controlling you little by little until there is barely any of you left.
» Living with OCD can be incredibly traumatic.

I can't begin to imagine how my mum felt that afternoon. Neither of us knew how to deal with the elephant in the room in Sainsbury's. There was a lot for her to process, and I didn't know what to say. I didn't want to talk about it with her. I was worried about what she was thinking and whether she thought she had done something wrong. Because, really, what on earth was wrong with me?

Neither of us knew. But for now, the promise of help filled me with a flickering flame of hope. I had no fear of being let down. Only a promise, which I clung to for dear life.

CHAPTER NINE

'Sometimes, all you can do is lie in bed,
and hope to fall asleep before you fall apart.'
—*William C Hannan*

Life begins to feel like a daze. I go through the motions, physically present, but growing more and more disconnected from my body and those around me. Each day is a battle, ending with me collapsing into bed, my emotions stunted and my body exhausted from panic.

I feel like I am in limbo. As the months pass by, I wake up each morning expecting today to be the day that my mum gets a phone call offering me help. But the promise of that day begins to get fainter and fainter, and in the meantime my OCD becomes increasingly embedded into my way of life.

Today is Monday. The worst day of the week. My 7 o'clock alarm jolts me awake. I smack the snooze button, crawling under my duvet cover like a badger burying itself in a burrow. I like badgers. Their burrows underground are huge tunnel systems, some up to 30 metres long. And some of them have been used for hundreds of years by different generations of badger families. Unfortunately, my bed isn't as impressive, but it is just as safe.

Simply the thought of another day ahead is exhausting. As usual, I ponder whether I should pretend that I am ill. It's not like I would have to put it on. The all too familiar feeling of nausea has already settled in my stomach, and my ribcage aches from the force of my heartbeat. If I thought hard enough, I could have a headache too. That is one of my superpowers, being able to think-on a headache.

I eventually force myself out of bed and into the bathroom. After using the toilet, I wash my hands three times. Then, I circle the outline of the mirror with my finger three times. I catch sight of myself in the reflection. My dull brown hair frames my grey face, dark circles under my eyes signalling my lack of sleep. I splash water on my cheeks, hoping to wake myself up a bit more. The cold is harsh against my skin.

I make it into school and sit in form time with Edie, Carys and Jasmin as usual. We are in Year 11 now, GCSEs looming ahead of us. This morning my friends are talking about Edie's birthday party. She will be 16. Being barely 15 myself, 16 to me sounds terrifying. The age of the teenagers I used to find incredibly intimidating as a child – and still do.

'You are coming, right?' Jasmin leans across the table, her new designer bracelet chiming as it brushes the table.

I nod. Edie was going to go out for dinner for her birthday, but now she is having a takeaway at her house. Because she knows that going out is too much for me, and that I will be able to come if it is at hers.

'We're getting Domino's.' Edie claps her hands, gleefully. Domino's is always our takeaway of choice.

I smile, shooting her a grateful look. I feel guilty that she has changed her plans, but I am also filled with gratitude for having such accommodating friends.

The bell soon sounds for period one. My first two lessons pass relatively smoothly. First is geography, where I sit next to Edie by the door. Just knowing I can get out easily if I need to reduces my anxiety. I try to stop my leg from jigging up and down, knowing it can be irritating for those next to me. In period two, I have a free lesson due to my reduced timetable, so I sit in the library flicking through my geography homework. The chatter of Year 7s at the computers nearby bothers me, but I manage to focus and get my homework done.

Breaktime arrives. I stay in my seat. The library is closed to the school at breaktimes, but my friends and I are given special privileges. Almost as if the library staff know that certain kids like us need it. I don't read as much anymore, but the library remains my safe space, albeit it in a different way.

'You feeling okay today?' Edie asks me between bites of her cereal bar. She is scanning the bookshelf for a book to read in half-term. She does not like my suggestions, so I have left her to it.

'I'm not sure,' I shrug. I feel the same as ever. Anxiety lines my stomach like poison, waiting to be called into action.

'Did you do the geography homework?' She knows that I spend my free periods working on the homework from the day. Our homework had looked complicated, but it hadn't been.

'Yeah. It didn't take long.'

'Good.' She nods, satisfied. We spend the rest of breaktime talking about our geography teacher's engagement, Edie's birthday party and the dress that she has just ordered online. Carys and Jasmin aren't with us – they queue up in the canteen for snacks instead, appearing at the end of break with a chocolate muffin and an Appletiser each. The look of the muffin makes my mouth water, but nothing is worth queueing up in the canteen for.

When the bell sounds for period three, anxiety swirls around my stomach. It feels like butterflies crashing against my skin, trying to escape. I bite my lip, willing it to stay at bay, and head out of the library to my French lesson.

I hate French. Not the subject itself, so much, though

languages do not come naturally to me like other subjects do. No, not the subject, but the class. The people who enjoy languages, like Carys and Edie, are all in a different set because they take two. Those of us who take only French have found ourselves in this set, filled with people who do not want to learn and just want to spend the hour cracking jokes and talking at the top of their lungs. To make matters worse, our teacher is on maternity leave and we have a cover who struggles to gain the attention of our class.

As always, I walk into the room and am hit instantly with mayhem. One of the boys dangles a girl's pencil case out of the window and watches as the pencils drop to the ground below. She tearfully runs out of the classroom to collect them, the teacher barely giving a second glance as she rushes past. She tries to shush the class, but there are too many layers of voices to hear, and too many who do not care to listen, for her to be successful.

The work is written on the board, so I open my exercise book and begin to complete the tasks. It doesn't take long for my brain to freeze and for me to be unable to focus. My pulse quickens beat by beat, and I place my finger against my wrist to feel that it is beating at least twice as fast as it should be. I concentrate on my breath, willing it to slow down and to remain under my control. It does, for now.

My bare legs feel sticky against the plastic chair. It is a damp, autumnal day, but I am sweating. My skin peels off the chair as I shuffle to try to get more comfortable. My blazer is already off and I have no more layers to strip. So, I take a sip of water, letting the dampness fill my insides. I imagine it travelling to each organ, relaxing them and enabling them to function effectively.

The boy who dropped the girl's pencil case suddenly starts laughing, as if he were watching a comedy show. His laugh is not soft, nor pleasant. It pierces my ears. The 20 other voices layer on top, clashing like multiple radios blaring different channels at the same time. The scraping of chairs chimes in. Somewhere towards the back of the room someone is playing music on their phone.

The noise begins to get louder and louder. Or I think it does. I suddenly feel too trapped where I am sitting, squished between two other students who are, at least, getting on with their work. The teacher's voice is shrill and hoarse as she tries again to get the class's attention and fails miserably. I feel my own throat get tighter, making it harder for the air to reach my lungs.

I stand up, the chair grinding the floor as I do so. I fling myself out of the row of seats and towards the door. Throwing it open, I feel cold air blast my face at once. But the sound of the class behind me is still too much. Too loud.

My thoughts are racing, but also absent because I can't hear them. They are too fast, like race cars crashing into one another. The only feeling I can make out, because of how my body is feeling, is that I am not safe. This place is dangerous. And I need to get away. I must get away.

And so, I run. Whereas some days my legs might take me towards the safety of the library or perhaps Miss B's office, today they do not. Today, my legs keep moving. Today, I find myself sprinting breathless to the fields at the back of the school, where the woodland and the outside world lies beyond. Today, I feel like I am going to explode if I don't get away. So I run, and I run, and I run. I'm not sure where to. I just know I need to get away.

My eyelids are heavy, bruised. They flick open slowly. Light blinds me. Groggily, I try to focus my eyes on the room.

Slowly, it comes into focus and I see that my curtains are wide open, the window ajar and daylight streaming in. I crane my neck to my right, to my bedside table. The clock is facing away from me. I try to lean over to turn it around, but my body weighs a tonne of bricks beneath me, as if my skin has turned to lead overnight.

Confusion settles in my chest. I don't know what day it is. I don't know what time it is. Mum or Dad must have opened my curtains, but I didn't hear them, I don't think. Or did I? The sound of the window latch unclicking is familiar. My hand frees itself from under my duvet and reaches for my hair. It feels like straw between my fingers, unbrushed. I pull a piece of dirt away from my scalp and stare at it, beginning to recall the events of the previous night. Images of the trees surrounding me, the darkness, the flashing lights, come flooding back. Fear fills my stomach. What happened?

I shrug the duvet off me, looking down at my body. My pyjamas are damp from sweat. Red scrapes cover my legs, dry blood stuck to my skin. For a moment I think they are bruised, but the bruises brush away, dirt falling onto my sheet. I swing my legs over the side of my bed, feeling the carpet ground me. Then I haul myself up and wobble to the bathroom, my surroundings blurring as I move.

In the bathroom, I stare at my reflection. My eyes look swollen, half-covered by my bird's nest of hair. I run the tap and splash cold water on my face, in the hope my thoughts will become a little less scrambled.

When I close the bathroom door behind me, muffled voices sound up the staircase. I hear the kitchen door open and close with a gentle click, and Mum's face appears through the bannister. Her eyes, usually sea-blue, are tainted red, dark circles encasing them.

'Morning,' she says, her eyes hovering over the grazes on my legs.

'Morning,' I mumble, biting my cheek.

'Can you put a jumper on and come downstairs? There is someone here to see you.'

My heart starts to race. 'Who?'

'A lady from a Targeted Youth Support team, I'm not sure exactly. Because you were missing.'

I stare at the floor as she disappears back down the stairs. I don't want to speak to anyone. I don't want to be told off. I didn't mean to run away from school. Or maybe I did. I don't really remember. I pull my purple Hollister jumper over my head and swap my pyjama shorts for a pair of black joggers. I catch sight of the clock. It is 1 o'clock. Thursday. I should be at school. In maths, I think.

I open the door into the kitchen and see my parents sat at the table with expressions on their faces that I can't quite read. A lady with long dark hair, probably in her thirties, is opposite them. She turns to face me and smiles.

'You must be Emily. My name is Samantha, but call me Sam. Sorry to have got you out of bed. I was hoping we could have a chat?'

I don't say anything. Mum gets out of her chair and moves to the fridge. She pours a glass of apple juice and places it on the table, in front of an empty seat, then looks at me expectantly. I sit down next to Sam. She's wearing a denim jacket, similar to one in my cupboard, and three bracelets dangle from her wrist. They chime together each time she moves.

'You're not in trouble, don't worry.' Sam smiles, her voice soft.

'Are you sure?' I ask, shifting my gaze to Mum and Dad. They both look tired. I wonder if they slept at all.

'You're not in trouble,' Dad repeats. He rubs his hands together on his lap.

'What about school? Have they said anything? Will I get a detention? Or be suspended?'

'No. They just want to know you're okay.'

I stare at the wooden cracks on our table. Some are natural breaks in the wood. Others are handcrafted with children's crayons and scissors. I run my finger over them, my broken skin from handwashing visible to everyone.

'Because you went missing, our service was informed, and I just have to talk to you about what happened. To make sure you're safe. Does that sound okay?' Sam asks gently, her hand poised over the paperwork waiting to be filled out.

It doesn't feel like I have a choice, so I nod.

'Can you tell me what happened yesterday?'

I look at Mum and Dad nervously. Then words start tumbling out of my mouth. 'I don't really remember. I'm sorry. I didn't mean to make you all worry. I just . . . I don't know what happened.'

Sam places a hand on mine. Her acrylic nails are blossom-pink, peeling at the edges. 'Take a deep breath. Why don't you start by telling me how the day started?'

I think back to the start of the day. The conversation about Edie's party in form. Breaktime. When Edie didn't like my suggestion to read *The Railway Children*. Then French. Yes, I remember being in a French lesson.

'Okay I can do that, I think.'

'Good. Let's just take it one step at a time.'

Taking things one step at a time was a mantra I began having to live my life by. Not so much out of choice, but because I could never predict panic. That conversation with Sam was the only conversation I had to have with the Targeted Youth Support team. They recognised that I was safe and me running away was merely an uncontrollable reaction to my anxiety.

Unfortunately, that incident wasn't the only time I ran away, though it is the one that stands out most in my memory. Perhaps because it was winter, and it was dark. Maybe I was missing for the longest time that day; I'm not sure. In those situations the hours would blend into minutes in my mind, panic having consumed me. One time I was found by a sixth-former down an overgrown alleyway behind the school. Another time the panic loosened its grip on me and I knew I needed help, so I found my way to a dog walker who called the school. Another time the helicopter came again.

I felt incredibly helpless. My brain was taking control of my mind and my body. I was putting my parents through agony each time and the worry of it happening again. I was forcing my friends to sit through interviews with policemen as they repeated the same questions. School staff were watching my every move like a hawk. I wanted desperately to return to the overly excited and eager Year 7 who won awards and whose name was not known by the entirety of the teaching staff.

The only good thing that came from all this (or so I thought) was that I was finally being offered some help.

I meet the lady who I am told is going to help me one rainy Tuesday afternoon at school. I am pulled out of class and taken into a small room next to the assistant headteacher's office. The room is dim and smells musty. Stale. There is a small oblong window near the ceiling, lathered in dust.

A lady is sat at a circular table that takes up most of the room. Warm blonde locks are pulled into a tight chignon bun at the nape of her neck. Tufts of hair stick out, unsettled by the wind.

She introduces herself to me as Penny, from the early-intervention service. CAMHS had declined my referral. Mum hadn't been very happy about it, especially after ten months on the waiting list. It had surprised me, because I thought they wouldn't want me to keep running away from school. But then Penny had called, saying she could offer me ten sessions of CBT-informed work. I hadn't heard of Cognitive Behavioural Therapy before, but I googled it immediately, of course.

Now, Penny pulls out a textbook of CBT exercises for children and young people. It is thick, and I wonder how we will get through it all in ten sessions. She flicks it open to the first page, then unzips her pencil case and opens a notebook to a blank page.

'I think it would be a good idea if we started by writing a list of some of the things that make you anxious.'

I shuffle uncomfortably in my seat. I have only just met her and I don't want to tell her what makes me feel anxious. 'I . . . I'm not sure. Everything seems to make me anxious, I think. Sometimes I don't know when I'm anxious and when I'm not.'

She peers over her glasses at me. 'When was the last time you had what you might call a panic attack?'

'At breaktime today in the canteen. That's why I don't like going in the canteen.'

'What do you think is going to happen if you do?'

'I'll have a panic attack, like earlier. It's too loud.'

I had crouched in the corner of the canteen by the water fountain, hands over my ears, eyes tightly closed, tears flooding my face. Cutlery clattered around me, high-pitched voices and shuffling of hordes of children freezing me to the spot. Miss B's voice had sounded in my ear, encouraging me to take deep breaths. After several minutes, I began to feel my legs again, and then followed her unsteadily to her office.

'Don't you think that a lot of people might feel like that going into the canteen?'

Thinking it's an absurd question, I look up at her. Her hair is thinning at the scalp, the blonde more subtle at the roots. Her lips are red. She looks a bit like an air hostess, dolled up ready for the flight.

'Not really because not everyone has panic attacks.'

'We don't know that.'

I stare at her, a look of pure bewilderment on my face. It isn't that I don't think other people experience anxiety; but I want her to help me with *my* anxiety, not theirs. And as far as I can remember, I have never seen any other student rocking in a ball in the corner of the canteen. Or anyone else being laughed about in class for 'faking anxiety for attention'.

'But everyone sees mine and it is embarrassing. And I worry about buying food from the canteen because it might be contaminated.'

'These are thoughts that a lot of people have. Let's plot them on this paper and then we can see how your thoughts might affect your behaviour.'

The end of the session can't come quick enough. I leave the room hastily and rush to the bathroom, where I lather my hands with soap and scrub them until they sting. I blink back tears as I wonder why – if everyone has thoughts like this – I can't seem to manage them.

That was seven or eight years ago, and I will admit that I can't remember word for word what was said in that meeting. But I do remember very clearly the irritation gradually building up throughout our sessions, until I felt the need to explode. I now know that Penny was attempting to use normalisation with me, a therapy technique used to try to normalise people's experiences to make them feel better about them. It didn't work. All it did was make me feel worse for feeling bad about things that apparently everyone experienced and just got on with without making a fuss. As a result, I felt less able to open up, fearing that whatever I said would be met with a statement of invalidation.

And, I felt that what I did say wasn't understood. Despite knowing that I hated unpredictability and change, she turned up at school randomly one day while I was in a history lesson. She wanted to see how I was at school without me knowing that she was going to come. Needless to say, I was very upset by her out-of-the-blue visit, and angry at her for thinking she had the right to turn up and be one of the many things that would likely ruin my day. I was taken out of my history lesson without warning to see her, to have one of our wonderful conversations.

A lot of emphasis was placed on my anxiety being caused by pressure that I put on myself to get good grades. And while, yes, I did strive for 100 per cent in exams, and revised for hours and hours on end, this was not the driving factor behind my anxiety. The driving factor was my perfectionism, my literality in that 'trying my best' to me meant spending every waking hour doing what I could to perfect my schoolwork, and the feeling that if I did something 'wrong', then something bad could happen. The intrusive thoughts and the compulsions, and my embedded drive to be perfect in everything, alongside the feeling that I just wasn't good enough, desperately needed tackling. Because life often felt unbearable.

I felt like I was being told that I was wrong for feeling different. That everyone else could manage their anxious thoughts but I couldn't. Even though I *was* different. She just didn't know it. Which was a shame. Because had she been taught how to recognise that, or had she really heard what I was saying, maybe some of what was to come might have been prevented.

After ten sessions, my time with Penny was over. I had to fill out some questionnaires, to measure my progress before and after Penny. I was very generous in my responses, afraid that I would be to blame if I hadn't made any improvements. And I had GCSEs looming ahead of me now, only a few months away. I had already started my eight-hour revision schedule on weekends and needed to dedicate myself fully to studying (just to be clear – this is *not* something I would recommend; it is very unhealthy). My panic attacks were slightly less frequent and my worries about germs had reduced. Maybe the work with Penny had helped slightly, but mostly it was because my brain had switched its fixation to studying, and I fought even harder to push away the anxious thoughts. So, I managed to turn my focus towards my exams and the long summer that loomed before me.

I can see my teenage self so clearly now, and I want to hug her so tightly and not let go. I can see her pain and suffering, how exhausted she is from trying to hold things together, and there is so much that I want to tell her.

To my undiagnosed autistic self,
I would love to tell you that you are autistic, because knowing that about yourself would take so much of your guilt and shame away. Unfortunately, you won't know that for a while, so for now I will tell you these things instead.
There is nothing about you that is wrong. Absolutely nothing. Every part of you is perfect. Even the parts you hate. ESPECIALLY the parts you hate, and the parts you wish were different.

You are not 'stupid'. You are comparing yourself with people whose brains are wired completely differently to yours. You see things exactly as they are. You will find people who understand you. Just hold on a little longer. I promise that you won't always feel this lonely.

I know that you feel different, and I know that feels incredibly isolating and horrible right now. I know you can't understand this, but one day that feeling of being different will be used for so much good. You won't always hate that feeling as much as you do now.

I know that the anxiety never goes away. I know that your brain never shuts off. I know you can't rid yourself of the feeling that you are broken, but there will be times when you are so full of joy that there will be no space for those feelings. You will learn that you aren't broken, in time.

It is okay to feel confused and overwhelmed. The world is a confusing and overwhelming place. What is not okay is keeping all those feelings inside of you. They are building up, bit by bit, and one day they will explode. Tell someone what things feel like for you.

You are so special. The things which you are mocked for are the things that make you so fierce, determined and loving. The people mocking you are in the wrong, not you. Hold on tight to who you are, to who you were made to be, and stay true to yourself in everything that you do.

It is true that this world is a hard one for you to be in. But it is not true that you are not meant to be in this world. There are things that will make your life easier, and then you will fight to make other people's lives easier. You must stay because the world needs you.

One day you will discover that you are autistic – and it will be the best thing in the world because you will finally understand. The more that you understand yourself, the more you will be able to piece yourself back together, piece by piece. One day you will flourish, as your authentic self, and it will feel wonderful.

Stay strong.

Love, my diagnosed autistic self

CHAPTER TEN

*'She's in
the clouds,
heavy and dark,
waiting to
fall like rain'*
—Christy Ann Martine

The day that I decide I am going to die is a Wednesday.

The decision comes into my mind already complete – and so casually, as if it were simply a choice about what I would have for dinner.

'Are you okay?' Mrs S, one of our sixth-form tutors, looks at me kindly. Her eyes are soft and sincere, green, the colour of emeralds.

Memories fill my head of being young, at Brownies, the girlguiding group, helping with cake sales and camp meals, the chaos not feeling so chaotic because she was there, leading us. Liked and admired by all – staff, parents, and girls alike. Our interactions during those years had been brief, but I can still smell the freshly baked cakes and hear the bustle around us. But, sitting in front of me now, leaning forward on her chair with her hands clasped together, she is a stranger.

I nod in reply, aware of my leg bouncing up and down like jelly. Panic no longer overwhelming me, shame and embarrassment take over. I feel my cheeks burn red, and I stare at the floor, uncomfortable. I think of my new English teacher, back in the classroom, confused at me having fled so suddenly, having muttered only the words, 'Sorry, I don't feel well.' She probably doesn't even know my name yet, as we're barely a week into the new school year.

'Are you sure?' she asks again, raising her eyebrows. She reaches for the tissue box beside her computer screen, pulling one out and passing it to me. It brushes against my hands, soft as a feather. I hadn't even realised that my cheeks were damp.

'Yes,' I manage to say. The words feel hoarse in my mouth, dry. I need water.

I am in fact not okay, but I can't share that with her. I am one young person in a sea of new Year 12s; I don't need to burden her. She doesn't even know me, and I don't know her.

'Do you want to talk about what happened?'

I shake my head, aware that the lack of conversation must be draining for her. I think she would like me to talk, but I feel only fury bubble inside my chest. This year was meant to be different. This was meant to be over.

Memories of the festival fill me. A dozen teenagers piling onto a minibus, me sitting next to one of the youth leaders on the journey, too anxious to engage. I had made the decision just four months earlier to join this church, desperate for a community, for acceptance, for understanding. Having grown up in a Christian family, I thought maybe this would be where I would find answers.

The festival itself was like nothing I had experienced before. Worship music blasting against my ears. A feeling of complete calmness. Surrounded by my youth group, new friendships having blossomed. Then me standing up, knees wobbling, walking to the front. A stranger placing their hand on my back, warming my skin. Then words of love and hope poured over me. When I walked away, a lightness I had not felt in the longest time engulfed me. Thoughts went to my stomach, empty from days of having not eaten, too afraid of food prepared outside of my home and unable to even think about filling my churning stomach. I went to my youth leader and asked to eat. She was taken aback. I told her it was okay. I wasn't anxious anymore. God had just healed me. This is what I had been looking for.

The following three weeks were the calmest I had ever felt. I felt filled with a Godly presence. Calmness shadowed me wherever I went. Every time I braced myself for the anxiety to appear, it didn't. I quickly adjusted and soaked in my newfound confidence. I went out with my friends to places I previously would have avoided. I chatted with the new students joining our school for sixth form, as if they were friends and not strangers. I felt myself flood with a warmth I wasn't used to; and breezed through each day, not dreading anything in particular. I was a new person. More confident. Happier. Ablaze with hope for the future.

But now, in this moment, sitting in this office at school, I realise that it's all been a lie.

The festival had lured me into a false sense of comfort. I had believed that God heals, and I had believed and wanted it so much that I had thought it true for myself. Thought that things could be different.

Sitting here now, awash with shame and fear, I recognise that living freely was too far out of my reach. I am destined to live with panic bubbling under the surface. Anxiety controlling me. Feeling suffocated by my own mind.

And then I know that I can't do it anymore. I know that it all needs to stop, forever.

Life wasn't designed for someone like me.

'Sorry, I'm okay now.' I breathe in deeply, standing up.

I don't want to talk. There is no longer any point in asking for help.

I made a decision that day that would change the course of my life forever. I stumbled into Mrs S's office, awash with panic, seeking comfort, only to realise I could not face another year of school like this. By the time I went to sleep that night, I was armed with a decision. The response I received from Mrs S was the kindest I could have asked for, but nothing she could have said or done would have changed what was to come. I didn't want anyone to know, so nobody would. My friends were distracted by the excitement of sixth-form life; my new teachers didn't know me so were never going to notice a change so subtle; and my parents would think I was just adjusting to a new routine.

But my brain was racing. Planning. Researching. Fixated on finding a way out.

The rest of that week felt impossible. My whole body was heavy in a way it had never been before. It was like dragging stone across concrete. Breathing became a chore. Dragging myself out of bed a marathon.

Once, I picked up the phone to call one of my youth leaders. I told her about my panic attack and how devastated I was. How God hadn't cured me. How this year was going to be just the same as last. I listened to her words. They were meant to be reassuring, but it was like they were hitting solid brick. I felt numb. Nothing anyone said would make me feel better.

For the first time ever, I didn't do my geography homework due on the Monday. Because I knew I wouldn't be there. I barely paid attention in class as my teacher explained it, my thoughts wandering elsewhere – to Saturday. I wonder now, what people would have thought if they could have read my mind.

On Friday night, I went out with my friend. We ate dinner and went to Tesco to buy cards. I didn't look both ways before crossing the road and laughed at the suggestion that I could have been killed. When we said goodbye, I hugged her. For just a second longer than usual. I said goodbye and told her I loved her, my words filled with a stronger meaning that she couldn't have deciphered at the time.

And then, on Saturday night, I attempted to take my life. For the first time.

A chill lingers in the air, the buoyancy of autumn not far off. There is a hum among the trees, the wind like a choir in the late evening. Somewhere across the lawn, a fox dashes between the bushes, its white-tipped brush a blur of red that just catches my eye. Behind me, laughter and music sound from the cabin, a party of 16-year-olds dancing, the remains of alcohol lacing their lips.

I move away from the group. I hold the can to my mouth; a dash of cider trickles down my throat. I haven't drunk very much – I need my thoughts to be clear – but the edge is ever so slightly taken off. Enough so that I can blame the alcohol if anything goes wrong. Enough so that the guilt doesn't overpower me.

This decision feels logical to me in this moment. My plans lie before me, just within my reach. Anxiety swirls around my stomach, like venom. I need it to stop. The idea of a tomorrow fills me with dread. I want there to be no more tomorrows. Only silence. Darkness. Limbo.

I briefly think of Edie, Carys and Jasmin, downing alcohol, and wonder what they will make of this. I know they will be sad, but I know that they will move on. They have their whole lives ahead of them. I try not to think of Mum and Dad. I just hope they will understand. They will be better off without me; and I hope that, with time, they will understand that too.

With a final glance back at the cabin, I disappear into the night, clinging to the shadows.

My heart breaks, to think of me back then. I was only a child, so broken, so hurting and so invisible.

I am not going to go into detail of what happened because that isn't helpful for you or for me – and ultimately, the facts of what happened don't really matter. I survived. I don't know why I am one of the lucky ones. I don't know why I got a second chance (and then a third) at a life that I didn't want to live, when so many others don't. I don't know why so many others who are loved just like I am don't survive. The world has lost so many beautiful souls.

Most days I wonder why *me*. Why am I more deserving than those who didn't get another chance?

The answer is, I am not. I was just lucky that day. Though I didn't see that for a long time.

CHAPTER ELEVEN

*'There comes a point where you no longer care if there's a light
at the end of the tunnel or not. You're just sick of the tunnel.'*
—*Ranata Suzuki*

It is the middle of September, but the leaves outside are already wilting, preparing for winter. Faint shades of orange are beginning to peep through the green, once luscious but now dulled.

A red-breasted robin hops from branch to branch, elegantly dancing in the breeze. It looks my way and pauses, then flies off, tauntingly. It is free. I watch its wings flap in the afternoon air, propelling it upwards, higher and higher, until the ridge of the window blocks it from my view.

The glass is covered in dusty fingerprints, reminiscent of child after child who has sat right where I am now. The window is not barred, but it may as well be. There is a dent in the bottom of the frame, probably from the foot of another inpatient desperately trying to escape.

Looking out over the garden, I feel an unfamiliar sense of peace. The clouds melt into the sky, like whisps of cotton. The trees sway gently in the wind. I long to feel it brush against my face.

Raised voices sound from the far end of the corridor, shaking me from my daze. I turn just as one of the girls bangs at the door, yelling to be let out. The noise is too much. I pull myself to my feet and move into the lounge, to sit on the edge of a worn sofa. There is a girl I don't yet know sitting on the sofa opposite. She has long blonde hair and she is reading *Little Women*. I would ask her how it is, but I am too tense. There is a lady sitting on the chair by the door. She follows me everywhere I go. Even into the loo.

All I can think about as I sit here is that I can't understand how my life has ended up like this. Where did I go wrong? Was there a specific day where the course of my life changed and led me to this point? Was it my grandfather dying that triggered my panic attacks that landed me in this situation? Or was I always destined to find myself here? Perhaps I am just broken.

That night, I lie on the stone-cold floor of my room. I can't get into my bed. I am being watched so I can't do my rituals. I would rather sleep down here anyway. The man sitting at my door keeps telling me to at least put my duvet over me, but I ignore him. His eyes are on me constantly and it is uncomfortable. Creepy, even. With each hour, there is a new person, and each says the same thing.

I don't want the duvet. I don't deserve the comfort, I tell them repeatedly. Eventually I turn over and ignore them.

Sleep takes hours to come. When it does, it is broken, fragmented, like shards of glass. My dreams do not bring comfort, only fear. Each nightmare shakes me awake, jolting me back to the darkness of my room. I don't feel safe. I wedge myself underneath the room's desk, ignoring the person at the door. I curl up into a foetal position, my knees rubbing against my chin. There, my legs stop shaking and I feel safer.

I wake early the next morning to sun streaming in through the flimsy blind. I draw it up but the room is not much brighter than before. It smells stale in here but the window can't be opened. I stare outside wistfully, noticing a rabbit hopping between clumps of grass. My eyes follow it until it disappears into the bush. I make a mental note to check for it again.

The person sat by my door follows my every movement. I hesitate, desperate for a shower. I move into the bathroom. They get up. I strip to my underwear, aware of their eyes boring into my skin. I switch on the water, feeling it soak me. Closing my eyes, I imagine myself under a waterfall, surrounded by beauty. I imagine what happiness might feel like. Or anything other than this emptiness consuming me.

Later that day, I meet with the psychologist for the first time. I am apprehensive at first, but she is a kind looking woman, dressed in a stripy black and white dress. She sits with her legs crossed, a green notebook resting on her knee, poised with a pen. I like her name – Ivy – and somehow that makes it feel easier to sit with her.

'How are you finding it here?' she asks.

I shuffle awkwardly on the armchair. It has purple cushions and a flowery back. The kind of pattern I would expect to see in an old people's home.

'I would like to go home,' I whisper, so quietly that for a moment I wonder if she has heard me.

'I know,' she replies sympathetically. Then she gestures to the shadow behind the door. 'Is it hard being on one-to-one?'

He stands outside the room we are in. Thankfully he does not have to come into therapy with me. He is just close by, in case Ivy the psychologist needs to call him.

I blink back tears as I nod vigorously. 'When can I come off it? I'm sure it is against my human rights.'

'When your doctor thinks you are safe.'

'I'm not going to do anything, I promise. I just don't want them staring at me,' I plead.

'It won't be long, if you stay safe. I'll ask your doctor to have a word with you.'

I nod, gratefully. Maybe I can convince him instead.

'I just wanted to meet with you briefly to get acquainted with one another. We don't have a lot to talk about today.' She changes the subject, eyeing my shaking legs. 'I imagine you must be exhausted from the past week.'

I bite my lip, memories flooding back in. The strangers staring down at me as I'd lain on the hospital bed. Their words sounding far away. The squeaky machine being wheeled towards me, the lady in a dark-blue tunic reaching for my wrist. I had squirmed and tried to pull away, but she had grabbed my sleeve and roughly pushed it up, strapping a tight piece of Velcro round my upper arm. Its tightness restricting my blood flow before eventually being released, allowing me to breathe a sigh of relief. My arm was left smelling like disinfectant from her grip as she walked away, leaving me with two other strange women.

They had wanted me to recount to them what happened. Not just the night that had landed me in hospital, but the years building up to it. So, I had gone through it, year by year, until we were at present day. Then I had told them that there was no reason for me to live. That everything was too painful. And nothing they said would change that.

I imagine that is why I have ended up here, sitting on this purple armchair in front of Ivy. My honesty and stubbornness has, as always, landed me in trouble.

She twiddles her pen with her fingers. 'I want you to tell me some of your reasons to stay alive.'

I stare at her in bewilderment. The reason I am in this place is because those reasons aren't enough. Nothing is enough to neutralise the pain.

'There are none,' I mutter, staring at the floor.

'There have to be some. Ponder on it for a while. Write them down and show me your list next time we meet.'

I don't say anything, but she seems satisfied that I will follow her instruction. I will, of course. I always follow instructions. She closes her notebook, an indication that our session has ended for the day.

REASONS TO STAY ALIVE*

» There are movies you haven't yet seen that will make you laugh.
» There are places you will go to that will fill you with awe.
» There are people you will meet who will fill your life with joy.
» There are things you will do that will fill you with purpose.
» There are books you haven't yet read that will fill you with questions.
» There is food you haven't yet tried that will taste like heaven.
» There are sunsets you will see that will fill you with wonder.
» The best moments of your life have not yet happened.
» There will be times in the future where you will laugh so hard you won't be able to breathe – and in those moments you will be so glad to be alive.
» Stay alive for future you, who is grateful that you made the choice to stay.

Love, a friend

---

* This is obviously not the list I wrote then. That list was much simpler, and included things like my dog, my family and my friends. Living for myself did not feel possible, so I had to try to live for other people instead. It didn't seem fair, at the time, especially as I thought they would be better off without me, but it was the best I could do.

I am pacing backwards and forwards, in my room. Number 9. I can hear screams, shouts and sobs. They are coming from my body, but I feel disconnected, like I am not in control. In my arms, held tight to my chest, is my diary. A green spiral notebook, with a painting of a rabbit on the front. Mum got it for me for my birthday. It has become my lifeline, somewhere to escape to. I write everything down in it. Everything that happens and everything that I am feeling. I never let it out of my sight.

'You have to give it to us, I'm sorry.' The support worker stands in front of me, her voice firm. She holds her hand out.

I eye my consultant, who is standing outside of my room in the corridor. I overhear him saying that I am being 'hysterical'. My eyes brim with tears. And anger. How dare he?

'Discharge me,' I demand. 'I'm not giving it to you.'

'The ring binder isn't safe. You're not allowed it, unfortunately.'

'I've had it for weeks. Nobody said anything. You could have told me this weeks ago and I could have used a different book. But I can't now. It's not finished.'

The support worker sighs. You don't understand, I tell her. Nobody understands, I tell her.

My efforts are in vain. After hours of crying and screaming, I am so exhausted and numb that I hand the book over. Then they leave me alone. I curl up on my bed, whimpering. I want all this emotion to stop. I want the pain to go. I feel like I am burning from the inside.

I harm myself. When I am found and my book is not returned to me, I demand to be discharged.

Later that day, I am holding a piece of paper and trying to process the words coming out of the staff member's mouth. She is sitting in front of me and my parents, in the visitor's room. She is a social worker, but she's not *my* social worker – because my social worker is on leave. I want to see her now. I like her. I like the way she talks to me; I like the clothes that she wears; I like that she knows things without me having to explain them.

I can't process what this lady is saying. I can only see the words on the paper I am holding: 'You are detained under Section 2 of the Mental Health Act (1983) for assessment and possible treatment of a mental health condition.' My name is written underneath it in bold letters.

I don't understand. I only wanted my diary. Then I wanted to go home. I didn't want to feel distressed anymore.

I am taken back onto the unit, more of a prisoner than I was before. I stare out of my bedroom window at the rabbits on the grass. I feel a pang of something in my chest. I realise it is fear. In a strange place, surrounded by strange people, I am more scared than I have ever been before.

The number of psychiatric inpatients who are autistic is shocking. In the UK in December 2022, this number was 1,280.[1] And that's only the autistic people who are recognised as such. We know that so many aren't. I wouldn't have been included in those figures. And neither would the other as-yet-undiagnosed autistic young people I was detained with.

As if these statistics weren't harsh enough, the average admission is five and a half years.[2] I can't begin to imagine the amount of trauma this must cause. Especially in a group of people who are already more likely to end their lives by suicide.[3] One study showed that this risk is even higher among late-diagnosed autistic adults;[4] then there is the number who die by suicide who may have been autistic without knowing.[5] Findings by Cassidy et al suggest that autistic people may account for 40 per cent of suicides, as there was evidence of elevated autistic traits in 41 per cent of those who completed suicide during the time period studied.[6]

Our society is failing autistic people in so many ways, but nothing shows it quite as starkly as these figures.

We are putting autistic people through hell – and when they break, if they survive, we put them *in* hell to try to manage their brokenness.

The system is unfit for purpose.

I know now that I was sectioned because I was autistic – and not only because of the impact of growing up undiagnosed and in a world that traumatised me. The act of sectioning was *literally* because I was autistic. Because I couldn't give up my diary, an object I had become so hyper-fixated on that I couldn't function without it. It gave me a routine I otherwise lacked and helped me to block out the overwhelming chaos around me. Taking it away from me removed the only remaining coping mechanism I had. I was left to process the comments from the people keeping me there that I was being over-dramatic and hysterical. I crumpled.

You see, psychiatric wards are not built for autistic people.[7] You could hardly design a better environment to enhance our stress – and yet we are placed there at our most vulnerable.

And, while this environment did manage to keep me somewhat safe, it is true that being there caused me immeasurable stress.

THINGS ABOUT PSYCHIATRIC UNITS THAT ARE STRESSFUL FOR AUTISTIC PEOPLE

» The loss of control.
» They are loud.
» The new surroundings.

» The unpredictability of the environment.
» The new people.
» They are very loud.
» Staff staring at you while you shower.
» The lack of normal routine.
» The lack of control over the sensory environment.
» Contracts that don't make sense.*
» The inflexibility over unit rules.
» Strangers touching all of your belongings.
» They are very, very loud.
» Being constantly misinterpreted.
» Things never go to schedule.
» Being unable to engage with your special interests.
» They are LOUD.

Day after day, I sit at the window watching the leaves change colour. Soon, stark shades of red and orange litter the ground so the grass is nowhere to be seen. It is the middle of October and autumn is now in full show.

'Emily, your family are here.' One of the nurses has stuck her head out of the office door and is calling down the corridor.

I get up slowly, my knees threatening to buckle underneath me. I have got over the initial dread of seeing my family, worried about what they must think, finding it painful to see my parents' emotion at me being here and not coming home

---

* For example, contracts stating 'I will not hurt myself'. When you have been admitted because of exactly that. When it is all your brain is screaming at you to do 24 hours a day. I, of course, true to my extremely stubborn ways, refused to sign such a contract when I was presented with one.

with them. Perhaps they have got used to it too and that is why it is easier. Today, though, will not be easy.

I walk to the end of the corridor, peering through the locked door towards the visitors' rooms. The door unclicks at the nurse's order, allowing me through. I take the five steps towards the room I am directed to and push open the door.

The smell of cleaning products hits me. These rooms have such a distinct smell, which will haunt me for years to come. I also smell pizza. Domino's, to be exact. A tomatoey barbecue smell wafts up my nostrils. Saliva fills my mouth.

'Hi,' I say, meekly.

Mum and Dad jump up from the sofa and hug me in turn. It feels uncomfortable and awkward, but I don't pull away. I know they need it. I stare at my brother and sister, 13 and 11, sitting on the sofa opposite. Thomas smiles at me weakly. Jessica glances at me, then throws open the pizza box.

'We got Domino's!' she says, cheerfully, shoving a piece into her mouth.

'I can see that!' I reply, trying to make my voice sound brighter than it is.

Unless they bring Coco, my six-month old puppy, the air feels heavy during our visits. Like we are avoiding an elephant in the room. Maybe that is the wrong expression. But we try and keep it light-hearted, even though the situation is anything but.

I gulp down three large slices of pizza, grateful for the change from cheap hospital food, which gets whisked down from the adult hospital across the car park and is usually cold and soggy by the time it reaches us.

The next hour drags by, the five of us grasping at straws for conversation. They don't normally all come together, but they have today because it will be a week before I next see them.

I try asking Jessica about school. She has just started Year 7. She doesn't say much. I feel guilty, wondering about the impact on her of me being here.

When the time draws closer to the end of our visiting slot, I feel tears prick at my eyes and an anger begin to burn in my chest. I try to avoid showing Mum and Dad my emotions. I try to bury them inside, feeling embarrassed and not wanting to add to their stress. This time, though, my body is rigid when they hug me goodbye. I barely look at them as they leave the building, with only two of their three children. A deep loneliness settles in the pit of my stomach. I wish, more than anything, I could go home with them.

Instead, I storm back onto the unit, tears flooding down my cheeks. My thoughts begin to race.

'What's wrong?' the nurse in charge asks me. I imagine she is internally groaning, waiting for me to kick off and cause her trouble.

I don't reply, running straight past her to the small lounge. Thankfully, it is empty. I crouch in the corner and cry hot tears, my cheeks burning. I feel my head whack against the wall. I wait for the pain to settle. I lunge at the sofa, punching it in anger.

I should be going to Devon with them. It is October. We always go to Devon in October. Except this time, my family will be going without me. It's my fault. I had encouraged them to go. I didn't want them to miss out. But it's still not fair. I shouldn't be here. I am furious at my doctors, at the staff, at everyone. At everything. At myself.

I feel my body shut down. I am making noise, I know. Loud noise. Screaming and crying and shouting. I can't control myself. There are staff in here with me, telling me I must go to my room because I am distressing others. But I don't move. I don't know why. I am rooted to the ground.

Then I feel two firm hands underneath my shoulders, pulling me up. I scream at them to get away. I am lifted, my legs swinging in the air, and dragged to my room by two support workers. It hurts. I know they aren't allowed to handle me like this. I tell them so. But they just leave, shutting my bedroom door behind me. They tell me I can't come out until I have calmed down. I curl up on my bed, consumed by distress. I wish I could just sleep and never wake up.

There is a lot about being on that unit that I can't share or talk about. It is impossible to convey the fear and the trauma that I experienced there. Some of the stories that I am going to share in the next few pages might not seem too bad – because, yes, I made friendships there; and, yes, there were some nice staff who really did help me. It may have saved my life. But I would ultimately leave the unit with more trauma and more nightmares than I went in with.

You would perhaps think that one positive of being admitted to a psychiatric unit is that undiagnosed autistic people would be recognised as autistic, and that this could help them to move forwards and learn to manage better.

Only, nope. That is wishful thinking.

Were my fixations, increased distress at disruptions to routine and change, intolerance for noise, rigidity in thought patterns and sensory sensitivities noticed?

Was my glaringly obvious distressed autistic state recognised?

Of course it wasn't.

And it wasn't even as though the question hadn't been raised.

*

The carpet is rough beneath my skin. I shuffle uncomfortably on the window ledge, twisting to face Grace. It is funny to think that I didn't even know her two months ago. Yet our bond has developed so quickly, I feel like I have known her forever.

Friendships in this place feel intense. There are 16 of us on the unit. All different ages, from different backgrounds, with different stories. And we have been put together, by no choice of our own, in the same place. This shared experience brings about a type of bond that nobody on the outside could quite understand.

Grace, Amelia and Phoebe have quickly become like sisters to me. We recognise each other's discomfort, sometimes before we recognise our own. We observe each other's day, from start to finish. We see the emotions that we all go through. We have the same desires: to get out of here; or, for some of us, to die. We know what that feeling is like, and that understanding brings comradeship. I know already that we will be friends for a long time. If we ever get out of here.

'How do you feel about home leave this weekend?' Grace asks me, fiddling with a tangle laced between her fingers.

I shrug. 'It will be weird, I guess.'

On Saturday I am going home for the first time in weeks. I had walked into my ward round on Thursday and practically begged my consultant to let me go. Home sickness has well and truly settled in, and I spend many hours of each day thinking about what it would be like if I went back, even for a short while. Thankfully, he agreed to three hours, with the long-term goal of building up to overnight leave. I am desperate for a breath of normality, something to bring me back to reality just for a little while. I miss Coco. But, at the same time, I am scared. Of the thoughts in my brain, and of feeling comfort when I don't deserve to.

'What do you think you'll do?' Grace asks, drawing a heart in the condensation on the window. I draw one next to hers.

I ponder over this for a moment. 'Have a shower with no one watching! Shave my legs. Pluck my eyebrows. Then watch Netflix with my dad. And Coco. We started watching *Once Upon a Time.*'

Grace laughs softly. Her laugh reveals her dimples, lighting up her face. She is pretty, there is no doubt about that. Her dark hair cradles her shoulders. There is a faint pink streak down her left side, remnants of hair dye. Her eyes are a deep brown, filled with kindness. But a deep sadness lingers there too.

'That's exactly what I do when I go on leave. Except watch Netflix with my mum.'

'What are you watching at the moment?'

'*Breaking Bad.* I love it.' Her eyes glisten. She has been in hospital nearly a year, transferred to her local unit here several months ago after a stint in a unit up north. She says it was nicer there. I can imagine that is true.

I am about to confess that I haven't heard of it, and ask if it is any good, when my doctor walks up to me. Not my consultant, but the speciality doctor who works for him. I find them both intimidating. In their hands lie decisions about my life, which makes me feel too powerless and them too powerful.

'Can I speak to you, Emily? About your question about autism?' he asks, gesturing to a side room.

My parents and I raised the question of autism with him a few days ago. My auntie has been pushing it, having noticed similarities between me and my cousin, diagnosed aged four. Truth be told, I thought the suggestion was absurd when I first thought about it. Until I met a girl on the unit who told me she had autism. To me she didn't seem to have autism in the way I usually envisaged it. Something about her made my thoughts shift. This girl and I were similar, I had to admit that. And I had heard that OCD and autism could be linked. Perhaps there was something in it. So, my parents had met with my consultant to talk about my childhood years. Now the speciality doctor was feeding back on that meeting.

'It's okay, you can say it here,' I say, too lazy to move into another room, and not wanting my conversation with Grace to be over.

'Okay. I don't think you are autistic; I think you just have high social anxiety,' he says, straightening his tie as he speaks. He towers above us, with an air of authority we will never feel.

I feel a quick pang of disappointment, but it passes quickly. My thoughts are elsewhere.

'Okay,' I say. 'Can I have my list back?'

He looks surprised, I think. Or maybe it's something else, I can't tell. 'Sure.'

He disappears and returns a moment later with a crumpled piece of paper. I look at it with disdain, irritated that he hasn't kept it neat. Some of the ink has run, as if water has been spilled over it. But the title is still clear: 'Reasons Why I Could Be Autistic', in black ink.

I wonder how many autistic people who were identified late wrote one of these lists. Because, really, is there anything more autistic than writing a list of the reasons why you think you could be autistic? You might as well just hand over a diagnosis to anyone with a list. With bonus points for references. I don't see how this could be any less reliable than our current diagnostic system.

My own list read something like this:

REASONS WHY I COULD BE AUTISTIC

- » I have always seemed to find things harder than other kids my age.
- » I am often confused by instructions.
- » I get overwhelmed easily.
- » There is a link between autism and OCD, which I suffer from.
- » I am a perfectionist.
- » I always need to be in control.
- » I struggle with change.
- » I grew up copying fictional characters to know how to behave in social situations.
- » I was bullied for not fitting in.
- » I am too anxious.
- » I don't like loud noises.
- » I struggle to wear certain materials.
- » I have always felt different, and I don't know why.

I like lists a lot. I think they are wonderful things. Practical, easy and pretty to look at. But that isn't why I wrote this list. I wrote it because I didn't think anyone would believe me unless I could justify exactly why I thought I could be autistic. So, I backed it up with research too (extra autism points for me there!).

Even before knowing I was autistic, I already had the urge to prove why it could be a possibility. A feeling that was destined to follow me through life. Because that is how our system works. Disabled people must constantly prove that they are disabled. For benefits, for accommodations, for support they need. With colleagues, managers, teachers, family members, in all kinds of home and workplace environments.

If we don't adequately prove it, we are denied support. We are told that we can't possibly be autistic because we don't *look* it (a statement that makes my eyes roll).

Hence, while writing my list, I also had a very different list in mind:

REASONS WHY I CAN'T BE AUTISTIC

- » I was a very well-behaved child.
- » I have lots of friends.
- » I make eye contact.
- » I don't like trains.
- » I am very empathetic.
- » It would have been noticed when I was a child.
- » I talk a lot.
- » I am loud.
- » I didn't miss any developmental milestones (in fact, in the overly high-achieving pattern I follow through life, I actually met most of them early).
- » I don't 'look' autistic.
- » I have a very vivid imagination.
- » I am creative.
- » I don't like maths or science.

This whole list is like a walking stereotype. But these reasons are often what stops someone feeling so lost and confused from knowing why. And when my doctor said he didn't think I had autism, these were the reasons I fell back on as to why he must be right.

It is 21 December 2017. Three months and two days since I first walked through the unit door.

Long red and green paper chains decorate the corridors, hours having been spent weaving them together. Because what else did we have to do? A small plastic Christmas tree sits in the recreational room, five small baubles hanging from it. Christmas music from the music channel blasts through the building.

Outside, the snow is no longer a twinkling white blanket, but instead a mushy brown pit, mixed with mud and rain. Yesterday morning I had woken to squeals from some of the younger girls. I emerged from my room to find flakes of snow fluttering down from the sky, sparkling in the sunlight. The girls were already outside trying to build a snowman, laughing as the snow melted in their hands.

For one day, the mood on the unit was mostly one of joy. Under the shower of snow, we were able to forget that we had been ripped away from our homes and locked in a ward. We were able to just be teenagers.

And that had been the most wonderful feeling.

The snowman still stands in the corner of the garden, now one-handed and slightly floppy. His other hand lays on the floor, having been blown about in the night. His nose, a carrot we stole from the staff fridge, has disappeared completely, leaving a dent in his face. Half of his body has melted away, droplets of water now on the ground. I don't think he will survive another night.

'How are you feeling?' Amelia appears at my side, squeezing my arm. There are dark circles under her eyes and a fresh graze on her forehead. I heard the panic alarm last night; it must have been for her.

'I'm okay,' I shrug, biting my lip. 'It's a weird feeling.'

Today is my discharge day. I look up at the clock on the lounge wall. A clock I have spent hours staring at, willing time to pass quicker. Time in this place feels frozen. Each day feels like a week, a week a month and a month a year. But the time *has* passed and now Mum and Dad will be here in half an hour to take me home. For good this time.

Over the last three months, young people have come and

gone. Phoebe left last week. Once I go, Grace and Amelia will be the last of the original girls from when I was admitted. I have sat at over a dozen discharge parties, each with their own chocolate or red velvet cake. Each time, I have sat at the dining-room table, trying to look pleased for them, but inside longing for it to be my turn.

Now it is.

'They're ready for you.' Grace bounds into the lounge, her curly hair swept backwards into a ponytail. She looks more upbeat, more energetic than usual. I wonder if she is putting it on for me.

I smile at her and Amelia, filled with gratitude that I hadn't had to make this journey alone. It would have been so much harder without their friendship. I think of the nights we sat out in the corridor, unable to sleep. Whispering to each other about what our lives were like before all of this. Refusing to listen to the nurse in charge telling us to go to bed, uncaring of the consequences the next day. It would be worth it, for just a bit of time in each other's company. Instead of lying awake, alone, in our dark rooms.

I follow Grace into the dining room. Some of the other young people are already gathered around tables. They are mostly new admissions; faces I am not very acquainted with. Staff members line the sides of the room. I wonder how many of these parties they have done.

My doctor coughs, stepping out into the middle of the room. Heads turn to him, expectantly.

'Emily, what can I say. Your time here has not been easy. There have been a lot of ups and downs. But you have come a long way since you were admitted. You bring a presence to the unit that will be missed, but you have a lot of potential and you will go far in life. Good luck with your A-levels and your continuing recovery with your community team.'

I nod a thank you at him, feeling slightly awkward that everyone's eyes are on me. I stand up and mumble a few words, thanking the staff for their help and the young people for their kindness and friendship. A few more staff members then speak, offering their congratulations and best wishes. I struggle to take in what is being said, my mind racing too fast. Most of me just wants to get out of here, but I have become so accustomed to being here that the change feels incredibly daunting.

Grace stands up, her turn to talk.

'I'm so glad that I met you, Emily.' She passes me a card. I open it, catching sight of several messages from the young people. I swallow hard. It is strange to think that in some ways, I will miss this community.

Grace then hands me a black marker pen. The moment I have been waiting for since I was admitted. I pull a chair to the wall and stand on it, stretching just enough to reach the top of the wall. I sign my name among the hundreds of others – Emily – in large letters, with the dates 19.09.2017–21.12.2017. Then I write #GiveMeMyBookBack. Laughter sounds from around the room. It has become a bit of a running joke, but inside I still feel hurt.

I leave the unit at 4.30pm. As Mum, Dad and I walk away, armed with bags and boxes of my belongings, I turn around and stare at the building for a moment. A rush of *something* floods me. The building that may have saved my life while at the same time adding layers of trauma and fear. I don't feel much different than I did when I was first admitted. Perhaps a little less angry at being alive. But I still feel different. Broken. And I still know that this world wasn't made for me.

That day, I left the unit, where I very clearly exhibited strong autistic behaviours, armed with diagnoses of

Generalised Anxiety Disorder and Mixed Personality Disorder – emotionally unstable and anankastic type (a.k.a. Obsessive-Compulsive Personality Disorder). I don't know how they could have got it so wrong when it was so obvious.

My safety plans listed the things I found hard with suggestions of how to deal with them. Something like this:

> Emily finds change difficult to manage – give Emily advanced warning of any changes that may occur.
> Emily finds it hard when she does not have a routine or structure to follow – help Emily to build up a routine.
> Emily finds loud noises distressing – help Emily to find quieter spaces and to use ear defenders when necessary.
> Emily can find social situations difficult to navigate – allow Emily extra time to process things.

Then, in 2022, I requested all of my notes, which the NHS Trust was obliged to give me under the Data Protection Act (2018). They arrived stacked high. Years and years of mental health assessments, reports and daily progress notes. And when I began to read them, I started to understand how they got it so wrong. They were never looking through other possible lenses. They chose one, the lens of me having a personality disorder, and made everything fit under that.

I had stared at the reams of pages listing autistic trait after autistic trait, with a few ADHD traits sprinkled in, and felt let down. How could nobody have noticed?

My meltdowns – which I'd experienced more frequently in the unit than during any other condensed period of time – were described as 'hysteric attacks when she does not get her way'. Reading that years later brought back all those feelings of being misunderstood. It broke me all over again.

Emotionally Unstable Personality Disorder, an illness

often arising from trauma, is a diagnosis commonly given to autistic people,[8] particularly autistic women.[9] It is an incredibly stigmatised illness, which it shouldn't be, but it is also frequently given incorrectly. It has symptoms of intense and unstable emotions, impulsive behaviour, anger, difficulty making and keeping relationships, recurrent suicidal behaviour and self-harm, efforts to avoid abandonment and chronic feelings of emptiness. You only have to meet five out of the nine criteria to be diagnosed. And this isn't really very difficult for an autistic person – especially when the criteria is subjective and biased towards the clinician's perspective in the first place.

Anankastic Personality Disorder (Obsessive-Compulsive Personality Disorder) has symptoms of extreme perfectionism, rigidity, order, neatness and inflexibility.

I can't for one second imagine how both of these could also describe a distressed autistic person in the midst of a mental health crisis. Though I guess that if I can be sarcastic, I can't be autistic.

Funnily enough, my notes from the unit school, dated within weeks of when I was first admitted, state that 'all staff have noticed a marked element of inflexibility in some of her thinking, and a very literal quality to some of her communication, which we believe may be worth investigating in a clinical context'. It is a shame that this wasn't given the attention it should have been, because that sounds like autism to me.

This is how autistic people are missed, time and time again.

This is how autistic children are failed by the systems around us.

Failed to the point that we do not want to live as ourselves.

CHAPTER TWELVE

'Do not waste time
pretending to be different things
to fit inside spaces too small
for you to spread your wings.'
—Cay

I am sat in an appointment room. I have sat in dozens – perhaps even a hundred – of these rooms since my discharge. Mostly, they are small and square with bright white walls that are harsh against my eyes, and contain simply a plain desk and two chairs. There is no life to them. But at least when the rooms get stuffy, the windows can be opened – a reminder that I am no longer trapped. The outside world is right there at my fingertips. It has been six months but sometimes I still wake up in a panic, afraid I am stuck and can't go home, only to realise that I am curled up in my own bed.

This room is different, however. It is dim, like candlelight; the bulb, housed within a green bowl hanging from the ceiling, provides little light. The early summer sun is on the other side of the building, and the canopy of trees blocks any sunlight there is. The window is slightly ajar, a chorus of birds sounding through the air. One briefly lands on the ledge, then takes off into the cocktail-blue sky.

We have ended up in this room because the question of autism has not gone away. The first psychiatrist I saw following my discharge immediately asked my mum, 'Has she been assessed for autism?' Although I'm sure this was based solely on the fact that I refused to go in to see her because she was not who I was expecting to see and I did not want to answer her questions. I stayed firmly in my seat in the waiting room instead. When she came out to talk to me, I don't think I looked her in the eye once. And now that I have begun to engage properly with my community CAMHS team, they also support the idea of an assessment.

My parents, still desperate for answers, and encouraged again by my aunt, who is adamant that I am not neurotypical, reached out to this private autism-assessment service. Even one of my sixth-form teachers has now suggested I could be autistic. The NHS waiting list is years long, so my parents have decided to pay for an assessment. We are privileged to be in a stable enough financial position to be able to do this.

That is how I have found myself sat here. Instead of plastic chairs, hard against my skin, I am sitting on a worn armchair, covered in what appears to be a hand-woven blanket. Mum and Dad sit on the copper-coloured sofa next to me. Opposite us, on dining-type chairs, are three women, all of a similar age.

The lady directly opposite me has just spoken. I stare at her. She is slightly older than my mum, her oval-shaped face beginning to show the lines of age. Her hair, once perhaps a shiny jet-black, is now dulled, strands of grey peeking out from underneath.

She is sitting with one leg over the other, one hand clutching her notebook and the other flopped over the side of the chair. She looks at me carefully, as if studying my expression.

I realise she has just spoken and that I haven't answered.

'Wha . . . what do you mean?' I stammer, my eyebrows scrunched up as I try to process what she has said.

She glances at her two colleagues sat either side of her. One of them – the one who took me into a different room to ask me countless questions and make me read the toad book aloud – is also looking at me. The other is flicking through reams of paperwork. I notice she puts a stash of my old school reports to the back of the pile.

'We think that there is one explanation for everything that you have gone through,' she begins slowly, her eyes moving between me, my mum and my dad. They sit there silently, my mum's own notebook sat open on her lap, her writing scrawled across the page.

'That explanation is autism.' She leans backwards, as if giving me more space to process.

I stare at her, wide-eyed. 'You . . . you think I'm autistic?'

She nods. Outside, two birds talk to one another.

'Are you sure?' I ask, confusion spreading through me as I recall the doctor in the corridor telling me I wasn't. The friends who told me I couldn't possibly be when I told them I was being assessed. Adults who said it would have been noticed when I was a child. My previous openness to the idea that I could be autistic had been clouded by others' doubts.

Yet, I have spent the past few hours having question after question thrown at me, being instructed to complete activities that I was sure weren't aimed at somebody my age and watching these women flick through school reports, questionnaires and my clinical notes.

One of them had asked me to pretend to brush my teeth, and to talk her through this as I did so. I had looked at her in bewilderment, indignantly telling her that I was not a seven-year-old child and that these activities were inappropriate for my age. But I had done it anyway. I had pretended to pick up a toothbrush from the table, acted out the gesture of putting toothpaste onto the brush and then mimed the motion of brushing my teeth.

To make matters worse, she had then given me a picture book of toads soaring across wetlands and towns, encountering a man, an old lady and a dog on their route. The book was wordless, and she had asked me to make up a story to it. She had originally told me the images were frogs but I had corrected her. They were toads, not frogs. Then I had sat there and stared at the pages, utterly perplexed about how this was going to establish whether or not I was autistic. Still, I did what she said. I made up stories for the pages, of the toads going on their adventure. Not without asking a dozen questions about how exactly she wanted me to do it, of course.

Afterwards, she had asked me lots of questions. I had sat at the table, my leg jigging up and down nervously, a fidget toy between my fingers.

'What do you think about being in a long-term relationship or getting married when you are older?'

I had shrugged. I can't remember exactly what I had said. Something about not being sure what the purpose of a relationship is, but that I wouldn't want to be alone forever. And most people get married, so I suppose that is what is expected. Then she'd asked me about how I know when I am feeling particular emotions. She had kept probing me for more, so I'm not sure my responses were adequate. And then questions about friendship, and my role as a friend. I think I did okay with those. I like to think I am a good friend.

I had answered all of their questions and completed all of their tasks. To assess whether I was autistic. And now, hours later, they have reached their conclusion.

I am staring at the three women in front of me, almost stunned.

'Yes, we are sure that you are autistic.' She smiles at me, as if conveying that everything would now be okay.

And in that one single moment, my whole world changes.

There is no doubt about it – that moment changed my life. I remember walking out of the building and staring up at the sky. It was cloudy outside now and there was a slight breeze against my face. I remember taking a deep breath and hearing her words over and over in my head. *One explanation for everything . . . autism.* Not a personality disorder, not simply generalised anxiety. But autism.

I did not really understand anything about autism at the time, beyond the little I'd learned in the unit, yet I suddenly understood everything about my life with a newfound clarity for the very first time.

This is by no means how every autistic person feels when they discover they are autistic. It is different for everyone. But, for me, there was an overwhelming relief at finally knowing. There was confusion about why it had taken so long. There was joy at knowing the truth. There was sadness for all the years I hadn't. And there was anger at the adults around me who hadn't noticed.

For the first time, in a very, very long time, I realised that I wasn't just 'stupid'. Everything wasn't my fault. In that moment, outside the building, I forgave myself a little bit for everything that had happened. I realised that I hated myself a little less. And I knew then that I had permission, finally, to stop hurting myself for everything that went wrong.

There was an answer that meant I could start to move on with my life.

Unfortunately, many autistic people are not given the same opportunity to access a diagnosis. Every autistic person who wants a diagnosis should be able to access one, within a reasonable timeframe.

Sadly, the diagnostic process is flawed.

The fact that the Autism-Spectrum Quotient (AQ), a screening tool designed to measure autism traits, includes the question 'Would you prefer to go to a museum or a theatre?' screams this.

I love the theatre. It is one of my favourite places. The buzz, the thrill, the excitement; it brings me a type of joy that radiates through my body and boosts my mood massively.

Museums, on the other hand, I often find too under-stimulating, too boring – of course depending on the type of museum. If I can hyper fixate on the topic, then that is wonderful. Provided people don't try to interrupt the day with other meaningless tasks.

This one question raises a dozen more for me. What is the museum? What is the theatre show? When am I going? Who am I going with? Where is the museum? Where is the theatre? What is the occasion?

All while knowing that to score an autism point I would have to tick 'prefers the museum'.

Looking deeper into the autism diagnostic process, you can see the flaws that impact the lives of thousands.

A happy autistic person is not likely to be diagnosed, because many of the behaviours leading to assessment are the result of distress and trauma. I was a well-behaved, high-achieving pupil at school. And I was a happy little girl. Despite all the other things that were troubling me, like my anxiety and OCD, I was never likely to be recognised. Instead, for me, it wasn't until my mental health significantly deteriorated that the autistic behaviours I had internalised and masked became more external and visible. The same will apply for many others like me.

It also didn't help that I was a girl.

WHY ARE AUTISTIC GIRLS LESS LIKELY TO BE RECOGNISED?[1]

» Assessment methods used for diagnosis have mostly all been developed from research into autistic cisgender males.

» Autistic girls may be told they are being 'hysterical' and 'melodramatic', or 'emotional' and 'hormonal'.

» Our autistic special interests tend to be more socially accepted – for example, reading or animals – but are still just as intense.[2]

» Autistic girls may feel more of an intense desire to fit in because of how we are socialised and the expectations put on us from a young age. This may make us more likely to mask autistic traits.[3]

» Many people still think of autism as more of a 'boy condition', so those assigned female at birth may be less likely to be referred for assessment.

» Autistic girls may be thought to just be 'shy' or 'anxious'.

As the above list states, our diagnostic assessments have been around for a while and were developed from research into autistic boys – because at the time, apparently, girls weren't autistic.

In Kanner's 1943 paper, eight of the eleven children were male.[4] And all of them were white. He ignored anyone who did not fully meet his rigid criteria – many of whom would later meet the criteria for Asperger's syndrome (removed from the *DSM-5* in 2013 as autism became recognised as a spectrum). This is a problematic diagnosis due to Hans Asperger's links with the Nazi Party and the idea that certain autistic people are superior to others.[5]

Asperger's cases were all boys. As reported in Silberman's book, Asperger stated he had 'never met a girl with the fully fledged picture of autism', suggesting that it was 'an extreme variant of male intelligence'.[6] Years later, Simon Baron-Cohen built on this idea, proposing the extreme male brain theory[7] and suggesting autism to be linked to high testosterone in the womb.[8] Much of the autism research completed during these years was based on white cisgender boys, meaning that autistic women, people marginalised for their gender and people of colour were rarely recognised.

In 1981, Lorna Wing, a pioneer in the autism world, discussed the lack of diagnosis of autistic women compared to men,[9] already suggesting that some autistic girls without learning disabilities may be missed due to their social and communication skills.[10] Sadly, this is still the case. Research has recently shown that girls are diagnosed on average six years later than boys,[11] with 80 per cent remaining undiagnosed at the age of 18.[12] More adult women are referred for assessment than men, too, which highlights the numbers that have been missed.[13] Thankfully this gap is the narrowest it has ever been, and hopefully the new generation of autistic girls will have a better chance of being recognised. However, the diagnostic process is still less likely to favour girls[14, 15] and the varied ratios of diagnosis between girls and boys in different areas of the UK is stark. In some areas just one girl is diagnosed for every thirty boys, but in other areas it is one girl to every two boys.[16] This shows the difference in understanding between different teams or referrers; and means that, sadly, so many are being let down.

The buildings that pass by the window are blurred. They stream by, one after the other, their blandness broken up by the vibrance of trees and bushes dancing in the breeze.

The car lurches over the speedbumps, tyres screeching indignantly. My body jolts, feeling the pressure from the door as I am pushed into it. We turn, onto the motorway, picking up speed. Now all I see is a flurry of green.

With one hand on the steering wheel, Dad leans forwards, fiddling with the radio station. It settles on a chat show. The sound of a low male voice, interrupted by squealing as guests join the show, sounds through the speakers. They are talking about the Brexit negotiations. I zone out, staring out the window at the hues of green beyond.

The lightness I had felt radiate through my body half an hour ago has faded. I had expected it to be met with mutuality by my parents, but instead there is silence, short replies and an air of heaviness.

Are they ashamed of me? I wonder. *Don't they see that this feels so right?*

I catch sight of Mum's expression in the rear-view mirror. I have never been good at deciphering her expressions, having often been snapped at for interpreting her as angry or bitter when she isn't.

To me, now, she looks forlorn. Her eyebrows are arched downwards – as are her rosy lips – and her eyes, usually a crystal-blue, are slightly lowered and murky grey.

Is she disappointed? Have I upset her?

I feel a wave of anger rush over me. They should be happy for me, like I am. They should understand that knowing this changes everything. I want to shout that it is a good thing, not a bad thing. We should be celebrating!

Is this the reaction I will be met with by everyone? I think of my friends, some of whom had been surprised when I said I was being assessed. One who had, at first, said I definitely wasn't autistic, but later shifted when I explained the reasons why I could be.

I decide to message her now. I open up my phone to a flood of messages from my psychology A-level group chat. It has taken months, but I am finally, to some extent, integrated back into sixth form. Having missed so much, I have dropped my third subject, geography. I think of Grandpa and hope he wouldn't be disappointed. At the moment, English literature and psychology are enough; and I study both with a deep interest, often finding myself extra work to do just because I enjoy it.

For the first time in my whole school life, I have found myself feeling safe at school. I have four teachers, two per subject, my sixth-form tutor and the SENCo. I don't find any of them intimidating, which is a big improvement on previous years. They don't make me feel anxious. I feel able to turn to them when I need support. And the difference it has made has been vast. I have not run away the whole year.

A message from my friend chimes through just as I go to text her. I slide the button to silent.

'I hope it all goes well today,' it reads, followed by three kisses.

I tap back a reply. 'Just found out I am autistic. Such a weird feeling.'

It takes less than three seconds for her reply to buzz through. 'Wow. That makes a lot of sense. Hope you're okay.'

I stare at the message. *That makes a lot of sense.* She is right. It does.

All the confusion, the overwhelm, the not fitting in, the misinterpreting people, the constant exhaustion from trying to figure everything out . . . it finally makes sense. I catch Dad's eye in the mirror. I can see his brain ticking at 100 miles an hour. He glances at Mum. I wonder if it makes sense to them.

I knew, from the moment that the words were said to me, that the 'label' of autism was the first label stuck on me that made sense. It was like a weight had been lifted. Like the dark clouds swirling above my head had been brushed away, leaving skies of clarity.

You see, I had a dozen labels put on me before that one. That is why the frequently asked question 'Do you really need a label?' when people request an autism assessment doesn't make the slightest bit of sense. We go about our lives collecting multiple negative labels before eventually finding out the truth.

LABELS I HAVE HAD PUT ON ME

- » Bookworm
- » Weird
- » Clever clogs
- » Bossy
- » Stupid
- » Drama queen
- » Party pooper
- » Gifted and talented

» Hysterical
» Over-dramatic
» Anxious
» Personality disordered
» Autistic

Receiving this final label made a world of difference in my own head. Not everyone feels this way at being diagnosed. Some are upset or angry with the diagnosis – that is completely valid too. But so is being happy.

And then, of course, those around us must process it too. I now know that my parents' initial reaction, of confusion and speechlessness, wasn't because they weren't proud to have an autistic daughter. It was because they were confused at how their daughter, who they had done their best to raise, had been autistic for nearly 17 years without them, or anyone else, knowing. Their understanding was still limited. They didn't know what being autistic meant, or what it meant for my future. Did it mean that my mental health would always be this bad? They didn't know what was autism and what was anxiety, what was autism and what was OCD or what was autism and what was depression.

So, while I sat in that car feeling like a weight had been lifted, for my parents it was 'What next?', 'How could I have missed this?', 'How did no one else notice?' and 'So, if my neurotypical daughter is really neurodivergent, what does this mean for her life?' We were in different headspaces. They couldn't see that receiving this diagnosis was everything that I needed in that moment. I didn't want to think ahead.

It wasn't their fault that they didn't really know anything back then. We left the assessment with a piece of paper, detailing a few books and websites we could turn to.

This is effectively what they say to you when you are diagnosed: 'Congratulations! You have just been diagnosed with autism. We can't offer you any support, but here is a list of resources!'

A VERY HELPFUL RESOURCE LIST TO COUNTERACT ANY NEED FOR SUPPORT*

YOUTUBE

Amazing Things Happen by Amazing Things Project
Welcome to the Autistic Community by the Autistic Self-Advocacy Network
How Autism Freed Me to Be Myself, a TedTalk by Rosie King
The Autistic Girls Network channel: *Building a Positive Space for your Autistic Child and/or Yourself* with Chris Bonnello, *Autism and Anxiety* with Dr Luke Beardon, *A Sensory Exploration of Being a Teenage Autistic Girl* with Joanna Grace

NON-FICTION BOOKS

The Spectrum Girl's Survival Guide: How to Grow Up Awesome and Autistic by Siena Castellon
Unmasked: The Ultimate Guide to ADHD, Autism and Neurodivergence by Ellie Middleton

---

* In all seriousness, I do recommend these brilliant resources, which are helpful for both autistic people, and those supporting us. This list is much better than the list I was provided with, if I may say so myself. It would be nice if people received some actual support, though, alongside a list.

Autistic and Black: Our Experiences of Growth, Progress and Empowerment by Kala Allen Omeiza

Queerly Autistic: The Ultimate Guide For LGBTQIA+ Teens On The Spectrum by Erin Ekins

All Tangled Up in Autism and Chronic Illness: A guide to navigating multiple conditions by Charli Clement

Different, Not Less: A Neurodivergent's Guide to Embracing Your True Self and Finding Your Happily Ever After by Chloé Hayden

So, I'm Autistic: An Introduction to Autism for Young Adults and Late Teens by Sarah O'Brien

A Different Sort of Normal by Abigail Balfe

The Autism Friendly Guide to Periods by Robyn Steward

Autism, Bullying and Me by Emily Lovegrove

Unmasking Autism: The Power of Embracing Our Hidden Neurodiversity by Dr Devon Price

Untypical: How the World Isn't Built for Autistic People and What We Should All Do About It by Pete Wharmby

The Reason I Jump by Naoki Higashida

FICTION BOOKS

A Kind of Spark by Elle McNicoll

The Cassandra Complex by Holly Smale

Geek Girl by Holly Smale

Frankie's World by Aoife Dooley

An Unkindness of Ghosts by Rivers Solomon

Eight Bright Lights by Sara Gibbs

OTHER RESOURCES

'Autism, Girls and Keeping It All Inside' by the Autistic Girls Network: autisticgirlsnetwork.org

Autistic Science Person website: autisticscienceperson. com/resources/

Autism, Identity and Me: A Practical Workbook to Empower Autistic Children and Young People Aged 10+ by Rebecca Duffus

Autism, Identity and Me: A Professional and Parent Guide to Support a Positive Understanding of Autistic Identity by Rebecca Duffus

Taking Off the Mask: Practical Exercises to Help Understand and Minimise the Effects of Autistic Camouflaging by Dr Hannah Belcher

So, armed with a diagnosis and a list of resources, I now had to decide who to tell. Deciding to disclose that you are autistic can be a very big decision. I sadly learned quite quickly that it made me vulnerable and opened me up to invalidating and degrading comments. And there is the possibility of people not seeing you the same way anymore.

But, for me, it didn't really feel like an option not to tell anyone. I was suddenly able to go, 'Hey, I am *so* sorry for that super-weird/awkward/embarrassing thing I did two years ago (that you have probably forgotten about but that I have never stopped dwelling on). Here's an explanation of *why*!' For this reason, I told my close friends immediately, via my private Instagram account that only 12 people followed. I posted an explanation of how autism in girls is different, because I knew not everyone would necessarily believe me. (I have since learned that this is not true: there are no 'male' or 'female' types of autism, just a whole load of stigma, prejudice, bias and societal pressures that affects the recognition and presentation of it.)

Some of the best (I'm being sarcastic, again) reactions came from adults. My particular favourites were: 'But she's so smart, how can she be autistic?' and 'Wow, she doesn't seem autistic at all.' None of these comments were made in bad faith or with bad intentions. But they shine a light on the lack of understanding among the general public. And, unfortunately, having to educate everyone when you have just been diagnosed is exhausting. I took it upon myself to educate everyone I could, not realising that it didn't have to be my responsibility.

Here are some tips on what not to say and what you could say, if someone tells you that they are autistic. Besides the maths one, all of these are comments I have received myself.

WHAT NOT TO SAY WHEN SOMEONE YOU KNOW IS DIAGNOSED WITH AUTISM

» But you don't look autistic.
» But my [insert relationship, usually 'nephew' or 'friend's son'] is autistic and you're nothing like them.
» Are you sure?
» Oh no, I'm so sorry.
» Everyone is a little bit autistic anyway!
» You seem normal, though.
» But you're not good at maths?
» You must be very high-functioning.

WHAT YOU COULD SAY WHEN SOMEONE YOU KNOW IS DIAGNOSED WITH AUTISM

» Thank you for telling me; I'm glad you felt able to share that with me.
» Is there anything specific you would like me to be aware of?
» What can I do to make things easier for you?

» Is there anything you would like me to understand?
» How are you feeling about your diagnosis?
» I am going to do my own research, because it is not your responsibility to educate me, but if there are any resources you think are good, I would love to look at those.
» I'm here for you if you want to discuss it, but I know you might be overwhelmed right now, so it's okay to take some time for yourself.

For a while after my diagnosis, I felt like I had everything I needed.

It was only as the months continued to pass and my mental health remained a challenge that I realised I perhaps needed something more than a diagnosis.

I needed support. I needed to understand what autism actually *was*, because to me all it meant was difference. And I still didn't know that difference wasn't a bad thing.

Unfortunately, autism-specific support is limited. Especially when you aren't a little kid anymore.

My relationship with my CAMHS worker continued to be built upon. I sat in the appointment room with her week after week, sometimes sullen and silent, sometimes cheerful and non-stop chattering. She listened and she helped.

I was privileged. I was surrounded by adults who guided me, and my diagnosis opened several doors of support. One of my favourite doors that it opened was a cupboard.

CHAPTER THIRTEEN

'We must be willing to let go of the life we have planned,
so as to have the life that is waiting for us.'
—Joseph Campbell

I hug my knees tightly to my chest, burying my head as far down as it will go. My heart hammers furiously against my ribcage. My breathing is fast and shallow, my chest too tight to expand fully, as if locked into place.

I feel the urge to hit my head against the wall, to feel the rush of blood to my forehead, the ache that will transport me back to reality. Although my thoughts are jumbled by the adrenaline, I know that I can't. I dig my fingertips into my arm instead, waiting for the sharp stab of pain. It comes at the same time as the relief.

I can't think clearly, but I can feel. Eyes closed, I focus on the hard tufted carpet beneath my feet, digging my heels into the ground. Each time my focus drifts back to the tightness in my chest and the rush of panic, I pull it back. To the soles of my feet on the fabric. To my shoulders forced up against the wall, cold and hard against my blazer.

The tightness begins to loosen. My breath gradually becomes slower and deeper. I know I am nearing the end of the tunnel. I just can't let it slip backwards, to consume me again.

My eyes flick open slowly, to the dust on the floor. I can't quite pull my head back yet, though; I am still frozen. I inhale through my nose, taking in the musty smell of old books and unfiltered air. My arm begins to loosen, and I reach out to press the walls around me. The familiar texture of rough wallpaper against my hands, less dry than they have been in years, but now covered in bruises, old and new.

I am safe, I whisper out loud, so quietly that I wonder if it was in my head.

My senses begin to adjust properly to my surroundings. The slight noise of children on the other side of the wall, their chairs squeaking as they raise their hands to answer questions. She is not here, so she must be teaching them. Otherwise, she would be sat in front of me, her soothing voice filling my ears.

I lean my head against the wall, exhausted but safe. In my cupboard. It can only be about eight square feet. Just enough to fit a cracked shelf, filled with old students' books that have been gathering dust for years. And fidget toys. I lean over and grab one now, selecting a small squishy caterpillar to squeeze. Its eyes bulge and I move my hands over the strands meant to be its legs. One falls off in my hands from the pressure. I put it back delicately, remembering the support worker who told me that they don't make fidget toys for my level of anxiety.

This cupboard is one of the reasons that I have stopped feeling the need to flee the school grounds whenever panic takes over. I just run here instead. Usually, small spaces make me feel claustrophobic, but here I am in control. My own space. A place of safety.

It's not *actually* my cupboard, of course. Though I seem to have claimed it as such. And if I think about it, it is probably not actually a cupboard. More like a storeroom. But we all call it the cupboard, and that suits me just fine.

The cupboard comes off a single classroom, in a small white building with four rooms. It reminds me of the little chalets we would hire on our holidays. The office is next door, with a window overlooking the cupboard. I sit with my back to it. I wonder who has been checking on me through it. Someone will have been. Someone always does. I can't leave a lesson without a dozen people being alerted.

Sometimes she comes in and sits with me as I calm down, encouraging me to breathe. Sometimes she is teaching, or busy, and I just come and sit here for as long as I need to.

I jump out of my skin as the bell suddenly sounds. A screeching noise piercing my ears. My hands immediately fly to my ears, gripping them tightly, and I wrap myself back into a ball. I rock back and forth until it is over.

You would think that here, in the special educational needs building, filled with autistic children with sensory problems, the bell wouldn't be the loudest bell on the school grounds. Yet, from my unvalidated research, I have established that it is.

There is a rush of chaos outside as the dozen or so children file out of the building onto the playground, to rejoin their peers. Breaktime. I decide I will not be leaving to go to the sixth-form building. Too loud and busy for today. I would rather stay in here, in my cocoon.

There is a soft knock on the door. Then it creaks open slowly. I shuffle backwards so she can enter. She smiles at me warmly and crouches down to sit next to me.

'Not a good morning?' she asks, tucking her short blonde bob behind her ear. She is wearing silver earrings, the shape of birds.

I shake my head vigorously, avoiding meeting her eyes. I pick at the floor, not caring that the dust is staining my palms.

'Shall we talk about it?'

Normally I don't like to, but we have agreed that I should, with her. To identify triggers. To look at ways that I can cope. To help me to understand more about when my brain switches.

I launch into an explanation of having been in my psychology lesson. I stumble across my words at first before they begin to flow. We have had many a conversation on the floor of this cupboard. Both of us fiddling with different fidget toys. She knows how to make me talk.

'Where is your book?'

I rummage in my bag and find it, handing it to her. A newer spiral-bound notebook, clothed in a beautiful purple fabric. She opens it onto the first page, which reads, 'What being autistic means to me'. It is decorated in multicoloured gel pen, with stickers and sequins lining the edges.

'You've made that look pretty,' she smiles. I am pleased that she likes it. It was the first page we looked at together.

This is my new book, filled with my thoughts, lists, resources, explanations. It is helping me to explore what autism is, properly for the first time.

It is possible that everything you already know about autism is wrong.

Everything I knew about autism before I was diagnosed was wrong. And if I, an autistic person who grew up not too long ago, can have such outdated, misconceived ideas of what autism is, then it is very probable that some of you reading this may also have those ideas. There are a lot of myths, many of which are still widely believed today.

AUTISM MYTHS AND TRUTHS

Autism is a condition that mainly affects boys. Historically this was thought to be the case. Hence, research was focused on boys (specifically cis white boys). Our understanding therefore evolved based on what autism looked like in this group. Anyone who didn't fit this category went unnoticed. As understanding has increased, the difference in the ratio of autistic boys to girls has narrowed.[1]

People have autism; they are not autistic. Although every autistic person will have their own language preferences, to many this idea suggests that autism is a negative thing. I wouldn't say, 'I have right-handedness'; I would say that 'I am right-handed'. Autism influences everything about us, and that is not a bad thing.

Autistic people lack imagination. Many autistic people are incredibly creative, imaginative and innovative, enjoying a variety of arts such as writing and acting.

Autistic people don't make eye contact. It is true that some do not, due to finding it uncomfortable or even painful. But it is not true that all autistic people don't. Some do, either due to masking or finding it okay. Some make too much eye contact!

Autistic people can't make or understand jokes. Sometimes some autistic people may not understand jokes, because our brains can be extremely literal, but autistic people can be hilarious (in fact, stand-up comedy is highly enjoyed by lots in the autistic community!).

Autistic people lack empathy. Although some do, some don't. Some feel it so intensely that it can be painful. We can struggle to recognise and understand other people's emotions, and relate to something we have not experienced, but this doesn't mean that we don't feel concern for them. The research on which this claim is based uses the Empathy Quotient, a self-report questionnaire shown to be flawed,[2] with many of the questions assessing social and communication differences rather than empathy.[3] Why not talk about the research that shows no difference in empathy levels between autistic and non-autistic people?[24] Or Damian Milton's double empathy theory, which suggests that the disconnect is between autistic people and non-autistic people, who see the world differently and have different life experiences?[25] Because higher rapport has been demonstrated among people with the same neurotype.[26]

Autistic people are good at maths. Hahaaa, hilarious suggestion. Some are, some aren't. Just like non-autistic people, we all vary in our likes, dislikes and abilities in different subjects.

Autistic people aren't social. Many do find socialising difficult, but we seek connection and love just like any other human being. Some of us prefer being on our own, but some of us are actually HYPER-social!

Autism is a learning disability. This is not true. Around 40 per cent of autistic people have a co-occurring learning disability[7] (though this figure is probably lower considering there are likely many more undiagnosed autistic people without a learning disability), but autism itself is not one. It is a neurodevelopmental condition.

You can tell if someone is autistic by looking at them. This is definitely not true. Autism does not have a look, despite what media depictions may suggest. Besides, many of us are highly adept at masking, whether consciously or unconsciously.

Everyone is a 'little bit autistic'. You either have an autistic brain or you don't and it can be quite dismissive or invalidating for an autistic person to be told this. Just like neurotypical people might have some autistic traits (because these are human traits, after all – just experienced to different intensities), I have

some neurotypical traits and this does not make me
neurotypical, just as it does not make them autistic.
An autistic meltdown is like a tantrum. This is untrue. An
autistic meltdown is an involuntary response to being
overwhelmed or overstimulated.
**Autism is a linear spectrum, from 'more autistic' to 'less
autistic'.** The autism spectrum is more of a circle than
a straight line. The 'spectrum' does not mean that
everyone is somewhere on it; it means that every
autistic person experiences different autistic traits
at different intensities, and that these vary from day
to day. A person's position on the spectrum changes
sometimes hour to hour or even minute to minute.
Those considered 'severely autistic' are often autistic
people who also have learning disabilities or other
conditions that mean they have higher support needs.

So, what actually *is* autism?

Autism is a neurodevelopmental condition that impacts
how an individual sees, interprets, understands and responds
to the world around them.

It is currently diagnosed using the *DSM-5* (the Diagnostic
and Statistical Manual of Mental Disorders) or the *ICD-10*
(the International Classification of Diseases). This suggests
that autism is a disease or a mental disorder, but it isn't. It is a
different way of seeing and processing the world, that many
autistic people recognise as a disability but still not a disease.
Worse still, the criteria uses a framework of deficit, painting
the autistic person as having 'persistent deficits' (why not just
'differences'?), 'restricted' interests (why not just 'focused with
the ability to hyperfixate'?), and 'impaired' functioning (hence,
happy autistics are often undiagnosed, until they are distressed
and meet the criteria).

I want you to imagine for a moment that we described neurotypicals in such terms and placed the criteria in a manual of mental disorders. Surely, if having an autistic neurology belongs in such manuals, then having a neurotypical neurology should too.*

Neurotypical Spectrum Disorder is characterised by persistent deficits in understanding that people with different neurotypes may do things differently to them; a restricted, repetitive, inflexible need to show that their neurotype is the 'default' and 'standard' neurotype; and persistent difficulties in recognising that 'deficits' are not 'deficits', but simply differences.

How is that for a diagnostic criterion?

Deficits are only deficits if we perceive them to be less than the 'typical'. Autistic people may communicate and socialise differently. Some autistic people may use augmentative and alternative communication (AAC) to communicate, such as sign language, picture boards, writing, gestures or AAC devices – and this should not be considered useful only for non-speaking autistic people, since it can have benefits for all autistic people, and therefore shouldn't be a last resort or viewed negatively.[8] Some may prefer being on their own to socialising

---

* This is my (probably poor) attempt at satire. It is of course important that autistic people are recognised and diagnosed, because it is (in most people's eyes) a disability, and there is support that cannot be accessed without a diagnosis. Though I suppose I am quite sceptical of the fact this is the case, and of the medical model in general.

in groups. And you know what – that is okay. It's a difference. Not a deficit. A deficit is the lack of support for alternative communication styles in the world around that autistic person.

As for us having 'restrictive and repetitive interests', why do they have to be described this way? Why can't they be 'specific' and 'focused'? Our special interests mean that we can excel in certain areas of work and study related to our interests.[9] They can, in fact, be the opposite of a deficit.

Special interests can be like oxygen for autistic people. We need them to survive. They help us to navigate the world in a way that we can process and understand. When we are deprived of them, it is like being deprived of oxygen; so no wonder we become distressed.

To be diagnosed, our traits must 'limit and impair everyday functioning'.[10] In some ways this is understandable, because how can we ever be expected to thrive in a society not built for us? But do we actually know what a healthy, thriving autistic person looks like? In a world that caters for their sensory needs, works with their brains and not against them and doesn't judge them for being different? My functioning certainly wasn't impaired when I was a little girl, and that is probably why I wasn't diagnosed until I was 16. So many people are not diagnosed until they are at breaking point because we diagnose autism only in struggling and traumatised autistic people.

I wonder what a diagnostic checklist would look like for autistic people before they reach breaking point? Perhaps it would include some of these traits.

AUTISTIC TRAITS

» A love of some sensory things, and difficulty with others.
» Periods of not speaking, or periods of being hyperverbal.

» Exceptionally strong interests in particular topics.
» Thinking patterns that can be quite black and white.
» Finding social situations difficult to navigate.
» A need for routine, sameness and familiarity.
» Difficulty navigating change.
» Experiencing emotions intensely, including joy.
» An ability to hyperfocus on particular things of interest.
» Experiencing meltdowns or shutdowns or exhaustion after high social demands.*

You might not even recognise the phrase 'autistic traits' because they might have only been described to you as 'symptoms of autism' until now. A phrase with connotations of illness, disease, treatments and cures. A phrase defined in the *Oxford Dictionary* as 'a change in your body or mind that shows you are not healthy . . . something bad'.

Autism is not bad. An autistic person is no less healthy than a non-autistic person.

I am NOT LESS than a non-autistic person because I am autistic. I am just DIFFERENT.

And DIFFERENT IS NOT LESS.

I have a different neurotype that means I have a collection of traits that differ to the majority neurotype. Some of these aren't spoken about very much at all.

LESS FREQUENTLY DISCUSSED AUTISTIC TRAITS

» Difficulty recognising people's faces.
» Having no verbal filter.

---

*　Though is this an autistic trait, or a result of being autistic in society?

» The 'autism accent'.*
» Difficulty with motor skills.†
» Talking too fast or too loudly.‡
» Extreme obedience, which can be detrimental to wellbeing.
» Lack of fear towards danger.§
» A better connection with animals than with people.

Most autistic traits aren't even mentioned in the diagnostic criteria, but we know they exist because we know about the shared experiences of autistic people. Although, of course, not all autistic people experience each trait. We are all different, all individuals and unique. We all have different combinations of autistic traits (and often ADHD traits too) and experience each one to different intensities.

One of my most absurd traits is bumping into people I apparently know on the street and not knowing who they

---

*   The autism accent isn't a legitimate professional term, though 'abnormal speech patterns' is, with autistic children having been recognised as often having 'abnormal' speech prosody and pitch.[11] The 'autism accent' has been coined by the autistic community. I don't know what is different specifically about our voices, but many of us have often been asked about our accent. I had my voice mocked as a child more times than I can count – another thing I tried to mask. Now I mainly just get told that I sound posh.

†   Though it may be that dyspraxia accounts for this, considering the much higher prevalence of dyspraxia among autistic people.[12]

‡   This is an ADHD trait. Whether it is an autism trait or not as well is debatable. It can be impossible to decipher where autism and ADHD start and end.

§   Again, for many people with ADHD, this can be because of high impulsivity levels, meaning that they simply don't think of the danger before acting.

are. (Not physically bumping into people, as one might expect the phrase to suggest, but rather just passing somebody you know . . . Hey, if neurotypicals can use this phrase, I can too.) Our interactions usually go something like this:

> Them: Emily! It's nice to see you!
> Me: [Does a double take, scanning them up and down and hoping something will click] Oh . . . hi!
> Them: How are you and your parents?
> Me: We're all good, thank you. How are you?
> Them: Yes, we're good. You must thank your parents for our Christmas card.
> Me: I will!
> Them: It was lovely to bump into you.
> Me: You too!
> Me: [left standing on the side of the road, utterly perplexed] *Well, that was one very worthwhile interaction.*

Prosopagnosia is 'face blindness', a condition where people can't recognise people's faces. I don't have this as such. I usually can recognise faces in day-to-day life. The issue arises more when I see someone out of context. Or if they change their hair. This crosses over into television shows and films. I will watch an entire film or TV series and still not be able to tell you what character is called what. My brain seems to recognise this information as unimportant, and it filters out anything that it doesn't think is essential.

My brain just doesn't seem to process information in the same way as other people's brains. I've known that since I was little, and now I know why. In some ways, my brain works extremely quickly, making links and connections at a fascinating speed. I am already thinking three conversation topics ahead in a conversation. I speak at such a speed to keep up with the pace of my brain. That is my ADHD, diagnosed only last year at the age of 21.

In other ways, I am told, I am very slow. 'For someone so smart, you are very slow' is something I have heard several times over the years. It seems that when you get 100 per cent in exams, despite these having content you can memorise, you are expected to have a lot of common sense and social skills. I have been told I lack common sense. I don't have a textbook to follow to navigate life. Hence why I always thought I was 'stupid' until I received my diagnosis. That explained all the hard stuff, but something that is often neglected is how a diagnosis can explain a lot of the *good* stuff too.

CHAPTER FOURTEEN

*'By being yourself you put something wonderful
in the world that was not there before.'*
—*Edwin Elliott*

Sparks of excitement rush through my body like electricity.
There is a skip in my step as I walk along the bricked pathway,
leaving the boat behind us. A two-tiered, cream-coloured
ferry, it floats magnificently in the water, a dazzling blue in the
bright sunshine. The horn sounds, signifying its departure.
It glides away across the lake, back towards the car park where
its next passengers await.

In front of me there are hordes of people, which makes me
feel slightly queasy. Some are clustered together in groups,
some pushing their way through the crowds. A little boy runs
past me making race car noises, crashing into my side and
almost toppling me over.

'Sorry!' he yelps as he disappears into the swarm.

I locate my family, who are slightly ahead of me, and brush
past person after person, all speaking different languages, to
catch up with them. I shudder as my skin brushes past others'.

The crowd leads us around flowerbeds, which are
surrounded by fern-green bars. They are filled with yellow,
purple and pink hues. In front of us stands a large building,
with a decorative white top displaying its clock. In its garden
are more flowers, shaped into the face of a mouse, its black ears
the centrepiece.

My own ears are filled with music, its tempo fast and its mood light. There are no words, but the beat uplifts us, a sort of radiance engulfing us. It is the sound of magic. My body wants to move, and I let it. In the past I would have held myself still, fighting the energy pounding to escape. But then I don't feel this. The freedom, the release of tension, the thrill. My arms flow at my sides, my shoulders sway. It is like dancing.

We now pass under an arch, the shade providing momentary blissful relief from the heat. The golden pillars stand tall, towering above us like watchful guards. And then we are out, into an open square, enclosed by a circle of brick buildings, yellow, red and blue, bordered in white, like icing on a wedding cake. Their porches impose themselves out onto the path, held up by dozens of pillars, indicative of their importance.

We wade through the crowd, all enchanted by the magic. But I am too eager. Sure enough, as we near the centre of the square, where a single tree stands propping up a flag, turrets appear, one by one. Tops of blue. Small, elegant windows. Towers appearing one at a time, until finally, it forms the shape of the castle.

I inhale slowly, entranced by its beauty. It beckons me.

'Look!' I squeal, clapping my hands, gleefully. I jump up and down, no other way for the excitement inside of my body to be let out. My plaited hair flicks against my bare shoulders.

'It's not that impressive,' Thomas sniffs, barely glancing at the castle, his eyes diverting to the group of young people standing near us. They are speaking German. 'I love that I can understand German.'

I roll my eyes dramatically. 'We've just got *here*, literally the most magical place in the world, and that is all you can say.'

He shrugs, a cheeky smile spreading across his lips, revealing his dimples. This is the second time we have been to Disney World, returning four years after our first trip. Last time we came I had persuaded him to wear Mickey Mouse ears too, like Jessica and I, but this time he has refused. His brown hair is slicked with gel instead.

The long road of tarmac stretches out before us, paving the way to the castle. Both sides of the road are lined with buildings, all with different purposes but grouped together to form the quaint-looking town. Bouquets of pink flowers hang from the windows, likely home to parties of bees and wasps.

I notice that Jessica is already distracted and gazing into a shop window to our left. Of course, the ice cream shop. It is a smaller building than the rest, with a striped awning reminding me of the sweet shop in Hope Cove. But the smell there, though sweet and syrupy, is nothing compared to the smell here. Wafts of fluffy candyfloss, freshly popped toffee popcorn, warm salted pretzels and an array of ice cream flavours surround us. It smells like heaven.

'We'll get one later,' Dad winks at Jessica. She moans, jokingly, and begrudgingly trots back over to us.

Behind us, there are squeals from excited children. I turn and reciprocate. Two large chipmunks are making their way out of one of the buildings, their feet flopping in front of them as they walk. Their bodies look soft; they are chocolate-brown, with cream tummies and faces. The one in front lightly taps the arm of the other as he cheekily reaches towards the flower baskets, making out like he is going to steal one. His brother hits his hand and he covers his mouth, as if to say, 'Oops, I got caught!'

'It's Chip and Dale!! Can we go to see them?' I screech, leaping into the air.

'If you stop squealing, then yes.' Dad winces at my pitch.

'Whoops, sorry,' I grin, then rush down to where the queue has formed.

The others stroll down the road slowly. By the time they

have reached me, the queue has doubled in length, but we are near the front. I stand impatiently, stifling the urge to stamp my foot like a child.

When it is our turn, the chipmunks greet us with wide arms and large smiles. Chip grabs onto my plaited hair and tugs it playfully. I expect Dale to hit his hand away again, but he copies, doing the same to Jessica. We all burst into laughter. A laugh so pure that I feel like I could combust from the joy. I clap my hands and spin in a circle excitedly.

I can't believe that I used to hide this feeling away. Feeling ashamed of the sparks that captivated my body. Suppressing the joy because it was 'too much' for other people. But not anymore. I bask in the joy, taking in every moment. It feels like magic.

I now know that the magic that pulsates through my veins is autistic joy, a truly beautiful phenomenon. Autistic joy is when the feeling of joy completely consumes you. You sink into it deeply; it radiates through you, like a warmth spreading through your body. Where everything around you melts away and all you can think about, focus on, or breathe in is the precipitator of the joy. It is like being transported into your own universe, where nothing else matters.

In those moments of joy, I forget who is watching and who is there. The joy is all I can see. I feel it with every bone in my body and express it in whatever way feels the best.

People don't always like to hear about the good parts of autism. To many people, it is still something bad and something that shouldn't be celebrated. But, just as autism makes my life hard at times, it can also be what makes it really good.

THINGS I LIKE ABOUT BEING AUTISTIC

» My strong sense of justice.

» My loyalty.

» It makes me like lists, and lists are great.

» My deep connection with animals.

» I do things in order, and that is the best way to do things.

» I see the world in all its vibrance.

» My honesty.

» My autistic sense of humour.

» Feeling that childlike excitement at small things.

» My ability to hyperfixate.

» The intensity with which I feel good emotions.

» My determination.

» The freeing feeling of stimming.

» Seeing things from a different perspective.

» I always see the good in people.

» I get so much joy from my special interests.

» Experiencing autistic joy.

» Autism IS me, and I am trying to like me.

I see the world in all of its vibrance. Even when things appear dull to others, they are bright to me. I am uplifted instantly by the sound of birds chirping. My whole body is warmed through by the brief passing of sunrays against my skin. I am sure that I can see more shades of green than other people do. My eyes are constantly searching, constantly awake. When I am not distracted, as is often the case, I notice the small things that other people don't. Like the twinkle of light in a sea of darkness. Or the comfort in familiarity.

My tendency to hyperfixate does distract me from my surroundings, but it can be wonderful. Being so engrossed in an activity or an interest that nothing can pull you away from is rejuvenating. Unless you forget to eat, pee or shower. Then perhaps not so much.

I like that I am honest. Honesty comes so naturally to me. Though it can cause problems some of the time (I have learned that not everyone appreciates honesty . . .), I am genuine. The look on my face before I remember to fix my expression reveals everything that I am feeling. My relationships are stronger, purer and realer. Small things do not build up inside of me the way they do for other people, because I can't hide how I am feeling. And apparently my honesty makes me funny.

A lot of people don't think that autistic people can be funny or understand jokes. But I am told that I am hilarious. I see the biggest smiles and the brightest laughs light up the faces of those that I love, and I get to know that it is because of me. It is a nice feeling.

What isn't a nice feeling is being judged and left out. But I know that because of this, I am a lot less judgemental than other people are. I give people the benefit of the doubt, like I wish I would be given when my facial expression contradicts my body language, or when I say something a little too abrupt. I want to make people feel good about themselves, so I try my hardest to do this every single day – and I like that about myself.

These are the things that make me proud to be autistic. The pride is not constant, especially on the hard days, but I am learning. Autism makes me who I am. And that (I am trying to believe) is a good thing.

Imagine if we described autism by this vividness, instead of its 'deficits'. Imagine if we built autistic people up by their strengths and not their difficulties.

THE VIVIDNESS OF AUTISM

Autism is not defined by an absence.
It is defined by a vividness.
I see the world in all its colours and sounds.
You see 20 shades of green. I see 200.
I notice the things that others don't.
It is chaotic, but it's vivid.
There is certainly no absence here.

This doesn't mean that the hard stuff doesn't exist. Of course it does. And people pushing the narrative that autism is a superpower and not a disability can be damaging. Autism never felt like my superpower, and hearing that it should be made me feel like my needs and difficulties were being ignored. I have learned, with time, that I can be proud to be autistic, knowing it is not a bad thing, while simultaneously understanding that it is a disability and can make my life harder.

Because, even with a diagnosis, darkness was never far away.

CHAPTER FIFTEEN

'The problem was never my mind;
it was a heart that could never hold all that it felt.'
—Shannon L Alder

This time, I know that it is coming. It arrives in the cold of mid-January, darker than before. Less forgiving. Depression stabs at my stomach, coiling itself around my veins and poisoning my blood like venom. It seeps into every part of my life.

I try to fight it at first. I cry for help – in fact I scream. But I am told that I do not qualify for intensive support because I haven't yet harmed myself. I do not go to school. Day after day, I sit at the kitchen table watching birds hop across the garden, envious of their carelessness and freedom. All I can do is sit there, completing jigsaw puzzle after jigsaw puzzle with my mum, tears pouring down my cheeks.

'Tomorrow will be a better day,' Mum tells me as she fits a piece of Simba's face into our puzzle of *The Lion King*. She is reassuring herself as much as she is me. 'Why don't we bake tomorrow? Nutella cookies – your favourite.'

We shouldn't be at home, counting down the hours until we can go to sleep. She should be at work and me at school, studying for A-levels. I imagine my friends gathered around the common room tables, playing card games in their lunchbreak. Jasmin will be winning, not understanding the game but winning anyway. Edie will be watching her in bewilderment, not understanding how. I wish, more than anything, I could be with them. Feeling better, not like this. They can't see me like this.

But how can this ever get better? My stomach physically hurts from the darkness. The thoughts stab my brain like a knife, telling me what I must do. So, I try calling out for help in my actions and not in my words.

Another short admission to the unit and months under the Home Treatment Team later, and I think maybe I am okay. I am shaken, fragile, but perhaps I can push through this. I sit my exams. Every day the weight of leaving school, my life changing and spinning out of control, hangs over me. Life changing to such an extent is something I cannot fathom. Not now, not just after school has become a safe place, and now it is being ripped from me.

The echo of noise bouncing off the sports hall walls creates a drumming in my ears. The low hum of air pumping into two bouncy castles is constant, interrupted by high-pitched laughter catapulting out of the mouths of a hundred young people. Some are gathered in packs, exchanging stories of the past seven years, posing for photos and signing yearbooks. Others are queuing up for the indoor inflatables, cheering and jesting at their friends.

The contrast of outfits is jolting. A group of boys from my GCSE maths class are in Teletubbies costumes, with halos on their heads and foil on their stomachs. Alice and her friends are dressed in red and white stripy T-shirts, blue jeans and white bobble hats, like Where's Wally. The range of characters are extensive, from superheroes to Scooby Doo, to Buzz Lightyear from *Toy Story*. The creativity is immense.

'Hello!' Edie bounds up to me in her Minion outfit, her yellow tights vibrant. 'Got caught up. You doing okay?'

I nod, gesturing to Jasmin on my left. She is dressed in a Piglet onesie, with me as Eeyore. 'She's counting down the minutes till we can get outta here.'

Jasmin groans. 'God, you make me sound like a right ungrateful pig. We're at the end now, it may as well be over. I wanna party.'

'You have plans after this? Besides McDonald's?' Edie raises her eyebrows.

'What is this – 21 questions?' Jasmin rolls her eyes. 'Right, you stay with Emily. I'm going to the loo.'

She marches off, pulling her hood over her head so the pink snout protrudes upwards. I stifle a chuckle.

'I don't need babysitting!' I call after her.

'It's not babysitting. It's moral support,' Edie says.

'Cause I'm a weirdo and don't want to leave school?'

'Jasmin would say yes to that. I wouldn't run that by her if I were you.'

Our conversation is interrupted by the blaring of a voice over a speaker. The deputy head, instructing us all to gather in the middle of the sports hall. One of the boys leaps off the inflatable, tumbling to the ground. Laughs erupt from his group.

Edie and I make our way to the middle, taking a seat on the floor at the edge of the group. Jasmin rushes over, wiping damp hands on her legs.

The head of sixth form begins talking. At first, I focus on her words. About how proud everyone is of us all. How hard we have worked and how we all deserve to achieve brilliant results in our A-levels. I look around the room, everyone's faces staring intently at her. Funny how seven years ago we were tiny eleven-year-olds. Completely unrecognisable to the group of young adults we are now.

This school building and these people have been normality.

Stability. When I think of different seasons, memories of different school years fill me. When I think of Jasmin, Edie and Carys, the majority of the time we have spent together has been here. Even though I've hated it, this is what I know and this is normal. And the thought of that changing is incomprehensible.

I catch the eye of my English teacher. She nods slightly, as if silently asking if I am okay. I pretend to ignore the cue, unsure if I've imagined it anyway, and look back to the front. My sixth-form tutor is now speaking, but her words sound jumbled up in my head. It's strange to think these adults who have guided me, and who I've turned to when I've needed support, will no longer be a part of my life. Edie and Jasmin, sat either side of me, no longer a regular part of my day. I can't imagine what a normal day will now look like without this, because I've never had to experience that.

I notice the feeling of my heartbeat. It is fast, and I wonder if this has just happened or if I've only now recognised it. What if the panic takes over? What if I suddenly can't breathe? The thought of the possibility turns my attention to my breath, and I realise I am right. It is taking effort to breathe. My palms are sweaty at my sides, my onesie suddenly an incubator, my body radiating heat far too intensely.

I know I need to move. If I don't, I will end up rocking on the floor right here in front of everyone. I can't bear the embarrassment of that again. Not today. My legs feel like jelly. I beg them to move, but it is too quiet; everyone will look. I need to move calmly, steadily, to the door – ten metres away. A heavy door that I will have to be able to pull to escape. *Move,* I will myself. *Move.*

Suddenly there is a round of applause, for a reason unbeknown to me, and I haul myself off the floor. To the door. Then I'm out of the hall, in a lobby. I pull open another door.

Into a small corridor. I unzip the top of my onesie and shrug my arms out, ignoring the bandages. I'm just desperate to be able to breathe. As I collapse against the wall and onto the floor, hands on my ears, the soft voice of my English teacher and tutor fill the corridor. Tears spill out of my eyes. The panic consumes me.

Midsummer, when the darkness finally stops swirling and settles in the pit of my stomach, I know that this time it will not lift.

This time is different. This time there is no getting through it. This time there will be no asking for help.

Just a final act.

It is dark. Light streams from the streetlights, illuminating the path in front of me. Cars pass by, not noticing the young woman lurking in the shadows. Somewhere in the distance a dog barks. I am numb. Crying, but numb.

I never wanted it to get to this point. I wanted to live life. I wanted to make my family proud.

But I know now that is not possible. I am broken. I will never be happy, and I do not deserve to be.

It is too painful. I need all of it to stop. And tonight, it will.

Depression lies. It tells you that you are not worthy. That nothing will ever get better. That you deserve to be in pain. These beliefs eat away at you, day after day, your brain in a constant battle. Unable to concentrate, complete mental exhaustion, withdrawing from your friends and family, more likely to become physically unwell. Until one day you surrender yourself to it.

Depression makes simply the thought of living too much to bear. Waking up every morning to the prospect of another day ahead of you is soul-destroying. Maybe you don't get up, but maybe you do. Plastering a smile on your face, hiding the truth.

Depression is dissociation. You might move through life, observing the things happening around you but feeling completely detached from them. You can almost watch yourself, disconnected from the memories being made and the emotions being felt. Nothing seems real.

Depression is self-destructive. It tells you it is okay to be in unsafe situations, to make impulsive decisions, to drink too much, to spend a lot of money. The future is non-existent. Nothing you do has any meaning.

Depression is physical too. The lack of appetite, or the opposite. The throbbing headaches. The stomach pain, a physical manifestation of your mind. Nausea. Missing your period. Weight gain and weight loss. Insomnia. It is all-consuming.

Depression triggers shame, guilt and anger. Overwhelming shame about not being able to do the things you used to, about not being able to look after yourself adequately, about being a failure. Guilt, about letting other people down, about not keeping your word, about not being the fun friend you used to be. Anger, at wasting valuable time. At not making progress. At being stuck.

Depression is saying that you are fine. Pretending. Getting dressed and ready for the day, going out as you usually would, acting like there isn't a war inside your brain. Being asked if you are okay and responding with, 'I'm fine'. Because, really, what else can you say?

Depression means the future is absent. You are unable to even contemplate the existence of a future, let alone plan for one. Perhaps you are already living in a future that didn't exist to you months ago.

Perhaps you know that today will be your last day.

Today is a day that shouldn't exist.

My body is screaming out in pain. My insides are burning. My head is pounding from the weight of carrying my body. I feel as if I have been stabbed, except I haven't been. The agony I am in is not physical, it is emotional. This is what I needed to stop.

My brain is murky. My thoughts don't quite make sense. I can't work out what is going on around me. The past week has been a whirlwind. Too many police, paramedics and doctors. Too many hours spent in a hospital. Too many questions asked of me.

I had lain on a hard blue mattress in a small side room of a hospital. The plastic squeaked every time I moved. Two police officers had sat in the armchairs opposite me, one a woman, one a man. They told me they were pleased I was with them alive and not dead. That it was far too close. Their words went over my head.

My friend had held me as I bawled, stroking my hair in reassurance.

'It will be okay. It's all going to be okay,' she had whispered, me rocking in her arms. Her body felt warm against mine.

'Why am I still here? I shouldn't be here,' I had choked through my sobs – although somewhere, in the back of my mind, a quiet thought began to wriggle its way to the surface.

I did not die. Even though I should have. Everything pointed towards this being impossible. Yet here I was, in the future that wasn't meant to exist. If this was so impossible, perhaps, just perhaps, I *was* meant to be here. Perhaps I should just try to move through the process of life and see what happens. And if it doesn't work out, then I could return to this darkness.

I decide that I will carry on as if the past week didn't happen. The section papers remain unsigned, a show of the strength of my dad's determination to convince the psychiatrist that hospital would only harm me, not help.

Now Dad is stood in front of me, leaning against the kitchen table. He looks tired, weary, older. His hair a shade greyer than last week. Mum is standing next to him, in a floral T-shirt and light denim jeans. Their mouths are moving, so why isn't sound coming out? Are they trying to tell me something? My brain is too overloaded, too overwhelmed. I try to focus, and the room comes back to life.

'Do you understand what we are saying, sweetie?' Dad asks, pushing his glasses up his nose. It is shiny with sweat.

I shake my head, tugging at the zip on my hoodie. My body is reacting as if I do but my brain hasn't quite caught up.

'They have said you can't go away with them,' Dad repeats, I realise for the third time.

'Whaa . . . what?' I stammer, my voice shaky. I am already crying. This must be why.

'You can't go to the festival,' Mum adds, her voice tainted with frustration. Her eyes shine.

'Why?' My voice sounds quiet, too quiet for me. My head begins to feel light, so I slide the kitchen chair out from the table and sit.

I can't understand why, because in this moment I can only see things from my perspective. I have attended my youth group every week for two years, now coming to the end as I have finished school. At a time when I had needed to be loved and accepted, I found a place among them. Structure, people who cared, new friendships that blossomed. Youth leaders who did their absolute best for me. I have felt cared for and wanted.

But this time they haven't messaged to see if I am okay. Maybe there have been too many times. Now there is just an email to my parents, taking away – in my eyes – not just a festival but a community that I have found to be healing.

Mum and Dad exchange a look. Then Dad speaks. 'They can't manage you.'

'But isn't there something they can do? Have they even asked? Can I not just go for the day? What if you came, like Italy?' Words spill out my mouth as I rack my brain for solutions.

'They are set on it. I'm sorry, Emily. There isn't anything we can do,' Mum says softly, crying now too. Dad fetches the box of tissues and offers it to us in turn.

Sadness and anger overwhelm me. At them, for not trying to make it possible. For making me feel like they have given up on me when I need them and for not contacting me. At myself, for being too difficult and too much. And now at not being able to say goodbye to my youth group.

Pain burns through my body, like real flames. If I wasn't autistic, I wouldn't feel this so intensely. If I wasn't autistic, my meltdowns and panic attacks wouldn't be so obvious and I wouldn't need so much support. If I wasn't autistic, I would be able to go away with my youth group because everything would be okay.

In this moment, I wish, more than anything, that I wasn't autistic. That I could just be normal.

Why couldn't I have been born normal?

It doesn't take long, once you realise that you are autistic, to begin to feel ashamed. Because all the things you've learned to hide about yourself are your unmasked, unfiltered, authentic autistic parts.

I still have a deep-rooted fear of allowing people to see the unmasked side of me. I fear that people seeing the 'autistic side of me' will make them leave. No matter how many times I am told to not be ashamed of my unfiltered 'joyful' responses to things, or my plain bluntness, or the stimming I suppress within myself, eight-year-old me whispers in my ear that I need to protect myself.

So, I try my hardest, most of the time, to not be 'too much', to not get overly excited and to pretend that I am not overwhelmed. I push away the meltdowns and the shutdowns as much as I can. All those memories of being teased for parts of myself I couldn't control are stored away in my memory, under lock and key. It is only with time, exhaustion, depleted energy supplies and having less desire to be controlled by what society expects of me that now that unmasked side of me peeks through a lot more often.

Unmasking does not always go well for autistic people. Especially when everything you do seems to be interpreted as rude.

THINGS I DO THAT ARE APPARENTLY RUDE

- » Asking too many questions.
- » Seeking clarification when given an instruction.
- » The tone of my voice.
- » Asking for a reason why I have to do something.
- » Being pedantic.
- » Questioning rules that don't make sense to me.
- » Putting things bluntly.*

---

* I want to say that being autistic of course doesn't give me, or any of us, a free pass. It does not mean we can just hurt people's feelings with bluntness. We must recognise when we do this

» Ignoring hierarchy when approaching a subject.
» Correcting someone on their mistakes.
» Struggling to let things go.
» Talking too much.
» Becoming fixated on something so being oblivious to things around me.
» Not being able to stop what I am doing until I have finished it.
» Not doing something I was expected to do even though I wasn't asked to do it.
» Not being able to do something asked of me.
» My mannerisms.
» Not giving eye contact.
» Avoiding a situation because it makes me anxious.
» Saying something is a fact, when apparently it's just an opinion.
» Not accepting other people's opinions, even when they are wrong.
» Not wanting to participate in social situations.
» My facial expressions.

The media doesn't help with our acceptance of ourselves. Storylines about autistic people almost always focus on how much of a burden the person is to their family and those around them because they are autistic. Look at Sheldon Cooper from *The Big Bang Theory*. No, he isn't explicitly stated to be autistic, but everyone knows he is. Pretty much the whole storyline is based on how irritating he is to other people. IN HIS OWN APARTMENT.

Why are autistic people's needs so often dismissed as

---

and take accountability for our actions. But sometimes being blunt is okay!

burdensome and problematic? If I need the lights dimmed because it is too bright and it doesn't bother anyone else, why am I such a nuisance? Why am I making out like I need *special treatment*? Then again, perhaps I do. Maybe my neurotype needs different accommodations, so why is the majority neurotype the one we must accommodate all the time? Why do I have to accept having bright lights on that burn my eyes just because somebody else likes having those lights to see what they are doing – even when they can see perfectly adequately with them ever so slightly dimmed?

Once you see how you are presented in the media, and how other people might view you, you can't unsee it. Once you have experienced being eight and everyone laughing at you for being 'weird', you can't *un*-experience it. Once you have spent your entire life trying to hide a part of yourself, you can't undo it.

It also doesn't take long, once you realise that you are autistic, to discover that there are a lot of people in the world who do not think that your life is valuable. It doesn't take long to discover the horrific abuse and murders that have happened to people in the not-so-distant past because they are autistic or disabled. It doesn't take long to find story after story of people discussing how burdensome you are, and how difficult you make life for other people.

Let's talk about Hans Asperger for a moment. An Austrian paediatrician who has, for a long while, been viewed as a pioneer in autism history. In 1944, one year after Leo Kanner published his definition of autism, Asperger published his, calling it 'autistic psychopathy'.[1] Like Kanner, he presented four case studies, describing the boys to be 'a particularly interesting and highly recognisable type of child'. This was published in German, and it was not until Lorna Wing described his work in the 1980s[2] that his ideas gained attention in English-speaking countries.[3]

In recent years, following Herwig Czech's discoveries,[4] and subsequently Edith Sheffer's groundbreaking book, *Asperger's Children*,[5] Asperger's links with the Nazi party have been revealed. These published works explain how Asperger sent hundreds of autistic children who he deemed to be unworthy to society (i.e., 'low-functioning') to Am Spiegelgrund, a clinic in Vienna, where they were experimented on and almost 800 were murdered. He signed papers for children to be sent there, describing them as 'unbearable burdens' to their parents. Some were starved. Some were given lethal injections. These murders were covered up as deaths attributed to illnesses like pneumonia. Those he thought were 'high-functioning' and intelligent, he protected.

I recognise my privilege in that I would likely be one of those 'high-functioning' children, but that still churns up so much anger within me. Our functioning abilities fluctuate. Autistic people's worth should not be based on how much we can contribute to society. Nobody's worth should be – yet that seems to be how disabled people's value is measured.

And, even today, so many autistic people are still depicted as a burden to society. In news reports and in media portrayals, again and again. There have been cases of autistic children being killed by their caregiver. Atrocious murders that should never happen. The responses to the news stories are mixed, but with far too much sympathising – the parents were exhausted and had too much to deal with as a parent of an autistic child; it wasn't their fault.

Filicide isn't uncommon. The Autistic Self-Advocacy Network state that 'in the past five years, over 550 people with disabilities have been murdered by their parents'.[6] The media often presents the parents or carers in a sympathetic light. The parent is given a relatively light sentence, if they are given one at all. The child is forgotten.

It is true that many parents and carers of disabled and/or autistic children are struggling, and it is true that there needs to be more support for them. But that never, ever justifies the murder of a child, or any disabled person.

I think about these autistic children and adults a lot. Those who are failed by the people meant to love them. Those who do not receive the support that they need and deserve. I know I am lucky for having been born into the family I was, and for receiving support when I am vulnerable. I am privileged because my lower support needs put me at less of a risk of these atrocities. But I hope that one day all autistic people will be well-supported, loved and valued for who they are.

'I hope that one day you know how loved and worthy you are.' Her voice is soft and delicate.

I tilt my head up slightly to look at her. She is sitting across from me as usual, one leg crossed over the other, her hands cupped on her knees. Her regular black heels, open at the toe to reveal her pink-coated toenails, point to the floor. Her fingernails are a matching rose-pink colour. I wonder if she is going on holiday.

My eyes move to her face. I can't read her expression. Neutral. Perhaps somewhat guarded, like she is hiding her emotions. Her eyes are blue like mine, slightly glassed over. My own are filling with tears. They meet briefly, then I look away, back to the floor.

I am quite accustomed to staring at this floor by now. It has been 18 months since I first sat in this chair. I know it is the same chair because one leg is slightly shorter than the other; it rocks from side to side as I shuffle. Momentarily, I wonder if she finds this irritating. Then my focus moves back to her statement.

'I know that I am loved,' I mumble. This is true. I do. I saw the brokenness in my dad's face when he realised that he had almost lost me. The exhaustion from helplessness in the creases on my mum's forehead. My sister's excitement when I walked back in the front door, instead of her having to visit me in hospital. The words of encouragement my friends constantly message me with. I know that I am loved.

'But it doesn't feel enough?' She cranes her neck slightly, possibly attempting to read my face.

I shrug, pulling at a loose thread off my jeans. I stare, pretending to be interested as a hole begins to form. She doesn't say anything. I realise she is waiting for me to respond.

'I feel like I don't deserve it. I feel like the pain is too much for it to mean anything. If they love me so much, why can't they just let me go?'

She nods slowly, registering my response. 'What about what you said to me earlier?'

I know immediately what she is referring to. I had walked into the room and announced that me being alive was impossible. That somebody, somewhere, must want me alive. 'That maybe there is a reason I am here?'

'Yes. Do you believe that?'

The clock on the wall ticks loudly, interjecting my thoughts. There are only two minutes left. 'I want to.'

'I'll take that, for now.' She smiles, gently. 'I am proud of you, you know. You have come a long way since we started working together.'

Tears fill my eyes again. I bow my head further, not wanting her to see.

'I know goodbyes are hard for you.'

A lump forms in my throat. It has taken me a long time to learn to trust her and open up. And now she is leaving like everyone else. Because tomorrow I turn 18. I have to move to adult services. And she is leaving anyway, for a new job in London.

'I don't understand how you can be sat in front of me now, and then I will never see you again.'

She reaches into her handbag, a worn, golden colour, and pulls out a small mirror. It is dark navy, covered in small, red flowers and outlines of little birds. It is no bigger than the palm of her hand. She extends her palm out to me now, gesturing for me to take it. I pick it up carefully. It feels smooth against my skin.

'Each meeting in our life is also a kind of meeting with ourselves.' I almost raise an eyebrow at her, her words floating completely over my head. 'I chose this little mirror for you because I hope when you look in it, you will see the Emily who has so many treasures, so many things to give to other people, family, friends, future friends and strangers, to whom you can give so much: your help, your smile, your super-smart ideas, your time, your generosity, your love, your care or just your fun. And you'll see that you'll also get back all these things from others. Because you deserve that, just because of who you are.'

There is no point me hiding my face now. I rub at my tears, realising my mascara has smudged. I must pull a face because she laughs at me.

'Thank you for helping me,' I manage to stammer.

'It was an honour. Enjoy your life. You have so much to offer.'

And with that, I say goodbye to the psychologist who has journeyed with me from 16 to 18, from in-patient to freedom, from childhood to almost adulthood. I walk out of the room, knowing that I will never see her again.

Later that evening, I sit on my bed in the comfort of my bedroom and pull the mirror out of my pocket. It feels cool against my warm hands. I imagine her having found it from a market stall, perhaps on holiday somewhere. Her hands moving from mirror to mirror until they had landed on this one. For whatever reason, this one spoke to her.

I unclick the latch, pulling back the top to reveal the mirror. A line of dust covers the rim. I brush it off gently, noticing the cracks on my hands. Have I been washing my hands too much again recently? I hadn't noticed.

I move the mirror away from me, allowing my face to fill the glass. Ocean-blue eyes stare back at me, a sparkle swimming somewhere beneath the depths. I study my cheekbones and jawline, wishing they were stronger, more defined. Freckles cover my cheeks, fainter than in childhood, but present nonetheless.

I think about what she said. All the gifts she believes I have to contribute to the world. Then I think of all my failures, all the times I have been a disappointment, all the times I have lost control. I try to shake them away. I have finished school now. My body is deeply unsettled by all the change, but I tell myself that this new chapter in my life doesn't have to be bad. I know that there are so many people who believe in me. I just wish I could start to believe in myself, too.

CHAPTER SIXTEEN

'Sometimes you have to drop your guard
so your heart can breathe.'
—*Emma Xu*

It is the day after my eighteenth birthday. It doesn't quite feel real that I have made it to eighteen. I am now an adult, no longer a child, yet I remain just as clueless, just as confused and just as inexperienced. I consider again the possibility that I am dreaming. Perhaps I will wake up, in heaven, or hell, following my attempt. Because how can I still be here?

I am jolted out of my thoughts as someone pushes past me. My body flinches. Their skin brushes against mine, exchanging beads of sweat. I keep my feet rooted firmly on the floor, nowhere else to move to. The stickiness of it, the remains of spilled sugary drinks stuck to the resin flooring, makes this easy.

'You all right?' Jasmin shouts over the noise. Her dark hair wraps around her shoulders, loose sparkles from her dress dancing in its waves.

'Yeah,' I shout back, tilting my head backwards to chug down more of my drink. The bitterness of the cheap vodka fills my mouth. The Coke masks the flavour enough for it to be neither particularly pleasant nor unpleasant.

I sway my hips as I shift from foot to foot, moving along in time with the beat. I wouldn't call this music. It is a series of sounds pressing hard against my eardrums. Usually this noise would send me straight into a panic or a meltdown, but the alcohol is helping with that. I do feel like I am standing on moving water, and the movement around me is ever so slightly blurred, but I am doing well. This is what normal 18-year-olds would be doing on results day.

I think of the envelope lying on the kitchen table back at home. I would probably prefer to be there with my family, though they will have retired to bed hours ago. I imagine the envelope still lies open, my parents proudly displaying the letters for everyone to see. An A* in psychology, an A* in English literature and an A* in my Extended Project Qualification, on whether the use of the Mental Health Act is an abuse of human rights. I think of the hours of work I put into that project, turning my anger into something productive, and feel pleased. I may have one fewer A-level than my peers, but I made it through school. Somehow.

'We done it!' I bellow at Jasmin, leaning closer to her.

'Done what?' She shouts back, her eyes half-closed as she dances.

'School!'

'Oh yeah! Cheers to us!'

Jasmin starts to push through the crowd further to the front. I grab onto her small shoulder bag, gold like her minidress, and follow her blindly. Her sequins catch the light from the disco ball, sending streaks of gold flying. They mix in with the multitude of coloured lights now flashing green and red all around us. I close my eyes to stop the lights burning, still holding on to Jasmin and inching forward carefully.

'Watch where you're going!' I feel the splash of wetness before I register his voice. My eyes flash open as the stickiness sinks into my skin. The man, who must be a few years older than me at least, tuts as Jasmin pulls me further away. I try to shake off the liquid, but it clings to me like a parasite. That will be me sticky for the rest of the night.

Jasmin finally stops. We are near the front. The DJ is a metre from us, elevated by the stage. He waves his arms in the air with the crowd. The noise here is deafening. I want to cover my ears with my hands, but I don't. I take another two sips from my drink instead, before feeling the final cold trickle go down my throat. I stare disappointed into the empty cup.

'Jasmin! Emily!' a slurred voice sounds from behind us. I spin around. The voice belongs to a girl from my psychology class. She beckons us to join a circle made up of a group of people from our school year. Usually I would edge away, making an excuse that I had to be somewhere else, but not tonight. Tonight, I am friendly. Eager to socialise. I shout a hello at them and join the circle, copying their movements as they jig from side to side. This is, I imagine, young people's definition of dancing.

The music changes to another song that sounds the same as the one before. I find my eyes growing heavy and my ears beginning to hurt from the noise.

'I'm going to get a drink!' I call to Jasmin, but she appears lost in her own world. I take in our surroundings so that I remember where to return to and dodge out of the crowd. No one even notices me disappear.

The bar is busy. It is lined with stools, but no one sits. There are just hordes of people gathered, people shouting out order after order, then having to repeat themselves to be heard. I join the back of the cluster, scanning for ways to get to the front. My eyelids suddenly feel like they weigh a ton, so I blink very rapidly to lighten them up. It doesn't work. My arms sway unknowingly at my sides, but each of my movements are heavier than normal. I think I might be drunk.

Eventually I reach the front of the bar. I lean on it, the stickiness cold against my bare arms. The barmen are all busy, but I call out anyway, banging my phone on the granite.

'Hello! Waiter!' My voice slurs.

They continue to busy themselves with other people's drinks. I tell myself I must be patient and wait my turn.

Then a voice sounds behind me. I turn around, intrigued.

'I recognise your voice,' I say, puzzled. I look the man up and down. His mousey-brown hair is dishevelled like his untrimmed beard. In his black trousers and tea-stained shirt, he looks like he has come straight from work. But he has trainers on his feet and Ray-Ban sunglasses sit on his head. It is not really a look I would have thought appropriate for a club.

'I don't know you,' I say slowly, scratching my chin. Then it clicks, and I announce, proudly, 'Ahh. You're the man who spilled your drink on me.'

He ignores my statement, squeezing next to me to plonk his arms on the bar. 'Do you want a drink?'

I stare at him in confusion. 'Why else would I be at the bar? Of course I am waiting for a drink.'

He smells of sweat and alcohol. I suppose I must smell the same. I notice that his collar isn't straight and tell him he should straighten it. He does.

'What do you want?' One of the barmen appears in front of us, a gleaming gold tooth in his grin.

'What do you drink?' the man next to me asks.

'Another double vodka-Coke please!' I shout to the barman.

'I'll have the same.'

When our drinks appear, I reach for the card machine to tap my phone but the man beats me to it.

'That was my drink, not yours!'

'I know.'

I look at him again, bewildered, then grab my drink and move away from the bar. I look towards the floor, searching for Jasmin and the group. But I can't remember if I came from the left or the right.

'Why did you walk away?' He appears at my side, again. I look at him, irritated.

'Because I got my drink.' I give him a stare, as if to say, *Are you stupid?* I have just decided that I want him to go away, when I feel my body being pulled towards him. His rough hand on my waist, then my lower back. I smell his breath at once. Before I even have time to gag, his lips are pressed against mine. Then his tongue is in my mouth. Touching my teeth, my tongue. I use all my strength to pull away. Then I walk off, ignoring his shout behind me.

I am shaken. The noise begins to get louder, decibel by decibel. I feel people getting closer and closer, and then, inevitably, my chest tightening. Tighter. Then my breath is shallowing, and within seconds I am aware that I don't feel safe. I run to the corner and crash to the floor, head down and knees pulled to my chest. I want to get out, but I'm trapped. I can't move. I can't breathe. Shouting sends me further and further away, until I feel a rough hand on my arm. I lash out.

'Oi! If you're too drunk, you have to get out of here!' The voice sounds far away. My eyes flicker open to blurriness, but I catch a lanyard hanging down in front of me. The person must work here.

I wrap myself up even tighter in the ball and rock backwards and forwards. I am in danger. I am not safe.

Then I hear her voice.

'She isn't drunk, she's autistic. Do you have somewhere quieter we can go?' It's Jasmin's voice. Relief washes over me. I know that I am safe.

★

I know that because I am autistic, I am more vulnerable than if I wasn't autistic. I know that this can be dangerous because I can be too trusting of strangers, I can shut down and be unable to communicate for myself, or I can find myself in dangerous situations.

Admitting this vulnerability can be a double-edged sword because sometimes this means non-autistic people jump in to try to protect us and help us without our permission, and without recognising that we have autonomy and are capable, much of the time, to protect ourselves. This can result in autistic adults being treated less like adults and more like children, which isn't okay. However, my vulnerability is a fact. And there are many reasons for it.

Autistic people, by nature, can be very trusting. While this can be a beautiful trait and mean it is easier for us to see the good in people, it can also cause us harm. The National Autistic Society found that half of autistic adults have been abused by somebody who they thought was their friend.[1] Maybe that is because we see the best in people. Or because we can't understand why anyone would hurt someone else intentionally, because we would never do that ourselves.

Autistic people are more likely to be bullied,[2] which makes us more vulnerable to experiencing depression, anxiety, despair and isolation.[3] Though there are many autistic people who do not abide by social expectations, the threat of being bullied may make some of us more likely to succumb to peer pressure. I was desperate to be liked and to fit in because I knew people saw me as different. I was lucky that my friends were relatively good influences on me, because for those of us who fall into different friendship groups, it can be easy to be led down the wrong path.

Then there is the fact that we are more vulnerable to

sexual assault. Autistic people are more likely to be sexually assaulted than non-autistic people, which is terribly sad. In fact, research suggests autistic women are between two to three times more likely to have been sexually assaulted than non-autistic women.[4] This could be because we may find it harder to understand social norms or recognise unsafe situations. Or because we are seen to be more vulnerable, so we are sought out. Or because we have found ourselves in 'unsafe' situations so many times that we don't know what is safe and what isn't. I spend most of my life feeling anxious, so how am I meant to recognise the warning signs when a situation would be seen as anxiety-provoking or dangerous for pretty much anyone?

Autistic people so often feel anxious socially that it can be hard to know when someone is crossing the line and acting in a way that would make most people feel uncomfortable. So many times, I have felt threatened or offended by things people have said that have turned out to be sarcastic and socially appropriate to other people. So, now, I tend to assume someone is being sarcastic and I have just misunderstood when this happens. Because I have been wrong – or have been told that I am wrong – so many times in the past, it can feel impossible to trust my instinct. When those danger alarm bells ring, the feeling can be so familiar that I am complacent.

I may not realise when I am being taken advantage of, especially if it involves someone with more authority. It's interesting, because a lot of autistic people do not see hierarchy as other people do, because it can lack reason and common sense. But, I have always had a major fear of authority figures and a fear of being told off. If I am told to do something by someone I see as 'in charge', I most likely will do it, unless I have a more critical hat on. I may not realise that there are exceptions to their instruction – for example, if I am feeling unwell, I may do it anyway.

All the vulnerabilities that we have as autistic people are different for each of us. But they are evident in the prevalence of mental health problems among us. We are vulnerable because we live in a society that traumatises us, just because we are autistic. Hence, 80 per cent of us experience mental health problems during our lives.[5] Autistic adults without a learning disability are 9 times more likely to die from suicide. Autistic children are 28 times more likely to think about or attempt suicide.[6] This is not okay.

Navigating life being more vulnerable because of all of these things can make life a hell of a lot harder.

MY ADVICE TO OTHER AUTISTIC PEOPLE

» Always tell someone you trust if someone else is making you feel uncomfortable. Talk it through with them.

» If someone is making you feel uncomfortable, even if you're 'misinterpreting' their behaviour, it is still not acceptable for them to make you feel this way.

» Stick to your boundaries. Don't let other people push these. If you are worried that they are too firm, talk them over with someone you trust.

» Don't put yourself in unfamiliar situations with strangers on your own.

» Before you do something that other people are doing, check in with yourself – does this act align with your morals? Does it seem right to you? Is it something you actually want to do, or are you just doing it because everyone else is?

» Ask yourself whether your 'friend' fits the definition of what you think a friend should be.

» You are not in the wrong for misinterpreting sarcasm. Something that makes you feel uncomfortable isn't okay just because it is sarcasm.

» Your instinct may feel unreliable and overly sensitive, but it is doing its best to keep you safe.

» You are not on your own, and you don't have to do things on your own because you feel a pressure to be 'independent' or 'responsible' for yourself. None of us is ever truly independent.*

» Some of us just need a bit more support than other humans, and that is okay, as long as your individual autonomy and capability is recognised as well, and you are in control of the support you receive.

I am lucky to have had a support system that held me upright. Family who fought for me when I couldn't fight for myself. Friends who defended me with every breath. My gratitude for them is endless, and I wish everybody was as lucky as I was.

'You're okay,' Jasmin rubs my back in circles with her hand, grounding me. I feel the press of her rings through my thin black dress.

I shiver, suddenly acutely aware of the cold. I lift my head from my knees and take in our surroundings. We are in a small, dark room, cramped from the sheer volume of boxes and coat racks. It is so dark that I can't see Jasmin's face properly, but even if it weren't for her voice, I would recognise the smell of her perfume anywhere. Fresh-cut flowers. A mix of lilies and roses.

---

* If we were, we would all live alone in shacks a hundred miles away from the next person.

'Where . . . where are we?' I croak, my voice still hoarse from the sobs. I swallow a few times, trying to force the lump in my throat to evaporate.

'I dunno. Some bodyguard put us in here. Said we could sit here as long as you need. I think I got the paramedic to go away.'

I raise my eyebrows. 'Bodyguard? Do you mean security guard?'

Jasmin laughs softly. 'I suppose so.'

I sigh, rubbing my temples. 'I'm sorry to have ruined your night. Again. I must have put you in this situation dozens of times over the years.'

I think of the number of times panic attacks have brought our evenings out to a halt. Restaurants, bowling alleys, even Edie's eighteenth birthday earlier this year. Somehow, far too often, I end up in the corner of a quiet room, crying and hyperventilating, dragging my friends away from the fun.

'Don't you dare apologise, Em. I don't think you get how much you've helped me too. I'd never have made it through school without you.'

I draw a deep breath. 'I can't believe it's over.'

Jasmin is silent a moment. 'Me either. What a relief.'

'I can't believe we'll never see each other every day again.'

I think of all the nights that felt just a little less impossible to get through because I knew I would see the smiling faces of Edie, Carys and Jasmin the following morning in form. And I knew, no matter what was going on in my brain, that somehow, they would make me laugh. And for a moment, everything would feel okay.

She pretends to punch me, playfully, her nails lightly scratching my arm. 'Don't put a dampener on the mood!'

'As if I haven't already,' I chuckle, gesturing to the room. 'We're meant to be clubbing!'

We both erupt into laughter, tension fading away from my body. She leans into me, resting her head on my shoulder. I gently push her dark locks away from my face, allowing them to cascade down her back in a myriad of curls.

'You didn't think you would make it, but you did. We both did,' she says, quietly.

'I'm scared about what's next,' I admit. The idea of a future, one I never thought I would have, is daunting.

'You don't need to be scared. You're gonna do great things, Em.'

I don't reply. Our bodies rise and fall rhythmically with each breath, in tune with one another. As I fiddle with the bracelet I am wearing, a silver chain Edie bought me for my eighteenth, I hope, more than anything, that Jasmin is right.

CHAPTER SEVENTEEN

*'You are not your past. You are the warrior that rose
above it to become the example of someone who
didn't just survive, but thrived in creating the
most beautiful last chapter of their life.'*
—*Shannon L Alder*

Today is the first day of the rest of my life. I have a chance to turn things around for myself. To put an end to the constant cycle of crisis. The prospect of giving up the destructive coping mechanisms I have had for so long and turning towards something healthier is difficult to comprehend. I don't know if it will be possible. But, I have decided that I will try. There must be a reason for me being here. So, what do I have to lose?

I pull my hair neatly to the back of my head and wrap the hairband around it. Hoping it doesn't look like a disaster, I check the mirror. I press my glossy lips against each other, tasting the sweet Lush lip scrub as I do so. The sugary taste runs to the back of my throat. I tilt my head to make sure my foundation and bronzer are blended properly. It would be terrible if I turned up looking like an Oompa Loompa. Those days of embarrassment are over.

As I grab my black bag from my desk and haul it over my shoulder, I am reminded of doing the same years earlier with my *Hannah Montana* satchel. I smile fondly as I remember my uncontained excitement at unwrapping it on my eighth birthday, believing it to be the best present of all time. How excited I was to use it on my first day of Year 4. Then the crushing disappointment and sadness when the other girls had got rid of theirs, and I was told it was now uncool. I could never keep up with them. Thankfully, now, I am learning I don't have to keep up with anyone. I have found many of my people. Those who support, encourage and love me unconditionally. And I have left much of that pettiness and nastiness behind me. As I quickly pull shut my bedroom door, I imagine giving my eight-year-old self a hug and telling her that it will all be okay.

'You ready?' Mum calls up the stairs, just as I appear. I wonder if she is as nervous as I am.

'You think I would be late?' I raise an eyebrow.

'I'm just checking!' She smiles, patting down her windswept hair. As if on cue, the dogs come bounding into the hallway, jumping up at my trousers with their damp paws. Coco licks my face, and I half-laugh, half-cringe.

'Coco! Kaia! Your feet need wiping!' Mum ushers them back to the door, where she grabs a towel and lifts their paws up one by one to pat them dry. Once Coco's are done, he leaps back over to me, rolling onto his back for a belly rub. I lean down and scratch him for a couple of moments before straightening up.

'Right. I best be off,' I say, sliding my shoes onto my feet and grabbing my car keys.

'Have a good day. Proud of you,' Mum smiles.

As I pull away in my small blue Fiat 500, she blows me kisses from the lounge window. I drive off along the tarmacked road, unsure if I am filled with trepidation, excitement, or anxiety. I feel my pulse racing and I will my anxiety to stay in check. I have never needed to be more in control, but I know that feeling that pressure will make me more likely to lose control and panic.

By the time I pull up into the car park, choosing a spot as close to the exit as possible, I can feel dampness on the back of my neck. I switch off the engine, the sound of Taylor Swift dying with it, and bury my head in my knees for a moment. I feel the rise and fall of my chest, the hardness of the floor beneath my feet, my back against the chair.

Just breathe. In and out. In and out. You've got this, I tell myself. *You may as well just try.*

I may as well as just try. Repeating the words over and over around my head, I open the car door and get out. The university building looms up ahead, towering above me unnervingly. Today is my first day as a student mental health nurse.

If I hadn't found out that I am autistic when I did, I am pretty certain that I would be dead. A fairly morbid thought, some might say. But it is true. Although my final attempt at ending my life was after I discovered this, my diagnosis allowed invaluable understanding to develop over the next few years of my life.

Finding out something so fundamental about yourself – like the fact that you have been living your whole life failing at being neurotypical when you are perfectly neurodivergent – takes a lot of processing. Probably a lot more processing than I ever realised it did – or can necessarily even comprehend now. I was, in some ways, incredibly lucky to have found out at the age of sixteen. So many autistic people, especially women, are now being diagnosed in their forties, fifties and even sixties. That is a lifetime of not knowing why you feel so different and a lifetime of not understanding.

Once I had learned that I was autistic, there was a lot of unlearning to do. Unlearning the belief I had that I was 'stupid', 'lacking common sense' and 'wrong'. Then, I had to apply myself to learn all of the things I never understood in the first place. The fundamental things, that children should grow up understanding. Like how their brain works. What coping strategies might work to make life slightly easier for them. Restructuring thought processes and expectations of myself.

I am still learning every day about how I can navigate this world in a way that is as stress-free for my brain as possible. Unfortunately, some of this comes down to the world being made more accessible. Why does music in restaurants need to be as loud as it is? Why do lights in shopping centres have to be quite so bright? Why do instructions have to be so unclear? Sometimes, when I disclose that I am autistic, I am helped with accessibility. But, sometimes the reaction is one of disbelief or belittlement.

It is no wonder so many autistic people don't disclose. It is often not safe for us to.

But, autistic people are everywhere. We are your healthcare providers, your teachers, your police, your gardeners . . . we are people you smile at in the street and people you chat to in the shopping centre. Sometimes you might recognise that someone is autistic, but a lot of the time, you won't. That doesn't mean that we aren't there.

It is impossible for someone to have never met an autistic person, because there are so many of us. You just haven't met an openly autistic person. Perhaps this is because that information does not matter in the context of the relationship, perhaps they are undiagnosed, or perhaps they don't want to disclose because of the fear of stigma and being misunderstood.

My greatest hope is that one day this will be no longer be the case.

★

I stare at my laptop screen, anxiously drumming my fingers on my desk. The all too familiar Zoom waiting room glares back at me. I've lost count of the number of Zoom calls I've been on now. Having never used it before, being accustomed to the familiarity of face-to-face interactions, this year everything we have known has been thrown into turmoil. The arrival of Covid-19 has thrown a spanner in the works of my first year of university.

Edie, Jasmin and Carys are home from university, but I can't see them. My own lectures are online. My placement has been cancelled. My whole routine is now chaos and the fear of death surrounding us catapults my brain into mayhem. But I am plodding on, soaking in the new content of my course and engaging with opportunities I am receiving online. It turns out, when a global pandemic stops you from leaving the house, you have a lot of time on your hands. And despite the challenges, I have been trying to use it to my advantage.

The screen suddenly glitches and the loading image turns into numerous small boxes, each bordering a face.

'Emily! Thank you so much for joining us,' Kate, the ward manager, beams.

I clear my throat, then unmute myself. 'Thank you so much for inviting me to talk today! I'm looking forward to it!'

'No need to thank us, it's our privilege to have you! Lots of us have been following you on Twitter, and we're so grateful you've given your time to us today!'

Twitter. A platform I have suddenly gained traction on. I started by tweeting about my diagnosis, and it soon became clear that a lot of people were interested in following my journey of self-discovery, as I learned more about autism and myself. And now people like Kate from this children's mental health unit have been reaching out to me, asking me to talk to them.

'So, thank you for inviting me to talk to you today. My name is Emily, I am 18 and a first-year student mental health nurse. I am also autistic and have been in a CAMHS unit myself. I hope some of the insights that I give you today are helpful.'

I spend the next hour talking them through my journey, the positives, the negatives, what helped and what didn't. I tell them about autism, and about what it's like being autistic for me. They all listen, engrossed, and when it's finished, they have a dozen questions.

After ten minutes, Kate raises her hand to silence everyone. 'Unfortunately, we have come to the end of our time. Emily, thank you. I'm sure I speak for everyone when I say how incredibly valuable that was. I know I am leaving here with a much better understanding of some of the autistic people we work with, and I am going to discuss with young people about implementing some of the ideas you suggested into their care plans.'

When the Zoom call ends and I am left in the silence of my bedroom, I sit quietly for a moment. I think over my journey, a flame beginning to burn in my chest. Anger at the injustice and the pain that autistic people are forced to endure. Grief for the years people spend undiagnosed and misunderstood. Sadness for all of those failed by the system. Desire for things to change for the future generation of autistic people. And hope, that I could be a small part of making that happen.

*

Dear the future generation of autistic people,

I hope that you are able to disclose that you are autistic, whenever and wherever you want to, without fearing repercussions, stigma, or disbelief.

I hope that your autistic peers who want to seek a diagnosis are able to, early, in a reasonable timeframe, and within a diagnostic system that is not belittling, but empowering.

I hope that when people think of autism, they don't think of the young cis white boy shown in every TV show with an autistic character, but instead of the autistic women, men and non-binary people, and people of every other gender and every ethnicity. I hope people think of autistic people who are transgender, indigenous and elderly; and I hope their idea of autism encompasses autistic people with varying levels of support needs.

I hope that autistic people are thriving in an education system that caters for their needs instead of forcing them to conform to a mould.

I hope that non-autistic people no longer make assumptions about what autistic people can and can't do, but instead look at every autistic person as an individual, with their own strengths, challenges, likes and dislikes.

I hope that people no longer assume that autistic people don't have romantic relationships, and understand that autistic people span the sexuality spectrum, just like they do.

I hope that 'autism hours' in supermarkets are no longer needed, because every hour becomes accessible for autistic people and all disabled people.

I hope that the rise in autism diagnoses is not criticised, with autistic people accused of hopping onto a 'fashion trend', and that instead society starts embracing the rainbow of neurodiversity.

I hope that being neurotypical isn't considered the default and 'standard' neurotype, to which all others are compared, and that autistic people aren't pushed to conform to this.

I hope that there is no longer a need to raise awareness, and that instead acceptance and understanding are widespread.

But most of all, I hope that you, and all autistic people, grow up valuing your differences, understanding your worth and loving yourself fully and unapologetically. I hope that you are a friend to yourself, because life is so much easier to navigate that way.

Love, an autistic person from a previous generation

EPILOGUE

The boy cowers behind the door, as if wishing the ground would swallow him whole. His small hands cover his body for protection, revealing the dried blood that stains his knuckles. The outline of a bruise is beginning to form and an indent in the wall suggests there has been an earlier outburst.

'Can I take a look at your hand?' I ask gently. I edge towards him slowly, but his hands begin to tremble. I back away, hands in the air. 'Okay. It's okay.'

He slowly shifts his face towards me. I see now that it is tear-stricken. Drained of all colour. His hazelnut eyes are wide and bloodshot, glazed over with fear. At his tender age of 11, they should be filled with twinkles of joy and mischief. But they are not – they are dull, because they have not seen laughter in too long.

I scan his room quickly, hoping to catch sight of something that indicates an interest of his that I could use to start a conversation. But the room is still unadorned and bare, as if waiting for its next patient. The cupboard lies empty, merely a hollow rectangle of wood. There is nothing on the small desk in the corner. The only signs of the room's inhabitant are the two plastic bags on the mattress, filled with a well-loved stuffed elephant, a pair of old trousers and a T-shirt. These things don't even look clean.

He is wearing his only other change of clothes. A plain red T-shirt that is the right size for his age but appears two sizes too big on his small body, and dark jeans, scuffed at the knees. He looks too small, too vulnerable to be here.

He should be at home, out playing with friends and wondering what his mother is cooking him for dinner. But instead, he is here.

I want to wrap my hands around his shaking body to comfort him, but I can't. I want to tell him that everything will be all right. I want to tell him that this is not the end for him. But he can't believe that right now. He is too wrapped up in the voices in his head. He only arrived three hours ago; he has a long way to go.

'It will be okay, you know,' I say. 'Eventually.'

His face appears to change shape. I can't read his expression properly, but I know it is not positive. I regret the words – how can I know it will be all right for him?

'You don't understand. You haven't been locked here.' He stares at the floor, his voice quiet.

I want to tell him that I understand more than he could ever know, but I don't. He is right – I don't know what he is experiencing. Instead, I sit down on the carpet next to him, watching the way his knee bobs up and down anxiously. I keep mine still. I always have to keep mine still. I must convey a sense of calmness. Then I tell him that we are here to help him – words which I have heard said to me so many times, and until now thought were empty. I tell him that it is okay not to trust us, and to feel the way he does.

'I don't expect you to trust us. And that is okay. But, I am going to be your named nurse while you're here, so I would really like to get to know you if you are okay with that.'

He shrugs, his fingers playing with a loose thread from his T-shirt. I take that as a sign to carry on.

'Why don't you tell me a bit about what you like doing?'

He is silent for a moment. Then a timid smile crosses his chapped lips. 'Can I tell you about my dog?'

I laugh softly. 'Of course you can! I am always very happy to talk about dogs!'

'Do you have a dog .. ?' He pauses, his eyes scanning my ID badge. 'Emily. Sorry, I forgot your name.'

'You don't need to say sorry. This can be a very overwhelming time. And yes, I do. I have two. What is your dog called?'

'Bruno. He's my best friend.' He begins to talk about Bruno, his Golden Retriever, and I notice his face lighting up slightly for the first time. Then a sense of sadness, as he remembers he won't be going home to Bruno tonight.

After five minutes of him talking about Bruno while I listen quietly, he stops and looks at me properly. A hint of caramel flickers in his eyes. 'I've been talking about him for ages. Normally people get annoyed with me and tell me to be quiet. Thank you for letting me talk about him.'

I smile, standing to my feet and straightening my tunic. 'We can talk about him whenever you like. I have to go and get the dining room ready for dinner, but it would be nice to see you down there in a bit. It might be nice for you to meet some of the others. But if you don't feel comfortable, that's okay too; I can bring your dinner here.'

I leave his room, propping his door slightly ajar so the support worker on his observations can see in. As I walk away, I can't help but think how lucky I am to get to work with children like him. It is hard being a nurse and being autistic. I require more support than others do, which is okay. I am well supported in my current role and learning that I do not have to fit into a box, which is what I grew up believing. I know there will be times I will burn out, and I may not manage it forever; but for now, I get to go to work and hear about special dogs like Bruno from incredible kids, many of whom are autistic too.

Autistic children deserve to grow up knowing how precious and wonderful they are. Feeling listened to and appreciated. Understanding that they are different, knowing why, and being properly supported to enable them to thrive. Too many of us are failed and it is time for that to change.

NOTES

Introduction

1. Atherton, G., Edisbury, E., Piovesan, A. & Cross, L. (2021). 'Autism through the ages: a mixed methods approach to understanding how age and age of diagnosis affects quality of life.' *Journal of Autism and Developmental Disorders, 52,* 3639–3654. https://doi.org/10.1007/s10803-021-05235-x

2. McCrossin, R. (2022). 'Finding the true number of females with autistic spectrum disorder by estimating the biases in initial recognition and clinical diagnosis.' *Children, 9*(2), 272. https://doi.org/10.3390/children9020272

3. Aylward, B. S., Gal-Szabo, D. A. & Taraman, S. (2021). 'Racial, ethnic, and sociodemographic disparities in diagnosis of children with autism spectrum disorder.' *Journal of Developmental and Behavioral Pediatrics, 42*(8), 682–689. https://doi.org/10.1097/DBP.0000000000000996

Chapter One

1. Kanner, L. (1943). 'Autistic disturbances of affective contact.' *Nervous Child, 2,* 217–250.

2. Kanner, L. (1944). 'Early infantile autism.' *The Journal of Pediatrics, 25,* 211–217. https://doi.org/10.1016/S0022-3476(44)80156-1

3. Bleuler E. (1950[1911]) *Dementia praecox or the group of Schizophrenias.* International Universities Press.

4. Folstien, S. & Rutter, M. (1977). 'Infantile autism: a genetic study of 21 twin pairs.' *Journal of Child Psychology and Psychiatry, 18*(4), 297–321. https://doi.org/10.1111/j.1469-7610.1977.tb00443.x.

5. Rutter, M. (1972). 'Childhood schizophrenia reconsidered.' *Journal of Autism and Developmental Disorders, 2*(4), 315–337. https://doi.org/10.1007/BF01537622

6. Wing, L. & Potter, D. (2002). 'The epidemiology of autistic spectrum disorders: is the prevalence rising?' *Mental Retardation and Developmental*

Disabilities Research Reviews, 8(3), 151–161. https://doi.org/10.1002/mrdd.10029.

7. Wing, L. & Gould, J. (1979). 'Severe impairments of social interaction and associated abnormalities in children: epidemiology and classification.' *Journal of Autism and Developmental Disorders, 9*(1), 11–29. https://doi.org/10.1007/BF01531288

8. Wing, L. (1981). 'Asperger's syndrome: a clinical account.' *Psychological Medicine, 11*(1), 115–129. https://doi.org/10.1017/S0033291700053332

9. Craig, J. & Baron-Cohen, S. (1999). 'Creativity and imagination in autism and asperger syndrome.' *Journal of Autism and Developmental Disorders, 29*(4), 319–326. https://doi.org/10.1023/a:1022163403479

10. Feinstein, A. (2010). *A History of Autism: Conversations with the Pioneers.* Wiley-Blackwell.

11. Li, J., Zhu, L. & Gummerum, M. (2014). 'The relationship between moral judgement and cooperation in children with high-functioning autism.' *Scientific Reports, 4,* Article 4314. https://doi.org/10.1038/srep04314

12. Cost, K. et al. (2021). '"Best things": parents describe their children with autism spectrum disorder over time.' *Journal of Autism and Developmental Disorders, 51,* 4560–4574. https://doi.org/10.1007/s10803-021-04890-4

13. Feinstein, A. (2010). *A History of Autism: Conversations with the Pioneers.* Wiley-Blackwell.

14. Rong, Y., Yang, C J., Jin, Y. & Wang, Y. (2021). 'Prevalence of attention-deficit/hyperactivity disorder in individuals with autism spectrum disorder: a meta-analysis.' *Research in Autism Spectrum Disorders, 83*(2021). https://doi.org/10.1016/j.rasd.2021.101759

Chapter Two

1. Sukhareva, G. E. (1925). *Shizoidynyee psixopatii v detskom vozraste* [Schizoid personality disorders of childhood]. *Voprosy pedologii i detskoĭ psikhonevrologii, 2nd edn.* 157–187.

2. Manouilenko, I. & Bejerot, S. (2015). 'Sukhareva – prior to Asperger and Canner.' *Nordic Journal of Psychiatry, 69*(6), 479–482. https://doi.org/10.3109/08039488.2015.1005022.

3. Silberman, S. (2015). *NeuroTribes: The legacy of autism and how to think smarter about people who think differently.* Allen & Unwin.

4. Zeldovich, L. (2018). *How history forgot the woman who defined autism.* Spectrum. https://www.spectrumnews.org/features/deep-dive/history-forgot-woman-defined-autism/

5. Wolff, S. (1996). 'The first account of the syndrome Asperger described?' *European Child and Adolescent Psychiatry, 5,* 119–132. https://doi.org/10.1007/BF00571671

6. Wing, 'Asperger's syndrome: a clinical account.'

7. Asperger, H. (1991). '"Autistic psychopathy" in childhood.' In U. Frith (Ed.), *Autism and Asperger Syndrome* (pp. 37–92). Cambridge University Press.

8. Silberman, *NeuroTribes.*

9. Zeldovich, *How history forgot the woman who defined autism.*

10. American Psychiatric Association. (2013). *Diagnostic and statistical manual of mental disorders* (5th ed.).

11. Turner-Brown, L. M., Lam, K. S. L., Holtsclaw, T. N., Dichter, G. S. & Bodfish, J. W. (2011). 'Phenomenology and measurement of circumscribed interests in autism spectrum disorders.' *Autism, 15*(4), 437–456. https://doi.org/10.1177/1362361310386507

12. Grove, R., Hoekstra, R. A., Wierda, M. & Begeer, S. (2018). 'Special interests and subjective wellbeing in autistic adults.' *Autism Research, 11*(5), 766–775. https://doi.org/10.1002/aur.1931

13. Nowell, K. P., Bernardin, C. J., Brown, C. & Kanne, S. (2020). 'Characterization of special interests in autism spectrum disorder: a brief review and pilot study using the special interests survey.' *Journal of Autism and Developmental Disorders, 51,* 2711–2724. https://doi.org/10.1007/s10803-020-04743-6

14. Amos, G. A., Byrne, G., Chouinard, P. A. & Godber, T. (2018). 'Autism traits, sensory over-responsivity, anxiety, and stress: a test of explanatory models.' *Journal of Autism and Developmental Disorders, 49,* 98–112. https://doi.org/10.1007/s10803-018-3695-6

15. Remington, A. & Fairnie, J. (2017). 'A sound advantage: increased auditory capacity in autism.' *Cognition, 166,* 459–465. https://doi.org/10.1016/j.cognition.2017.04.002

16. Brinkert, J. & Remington, A. (2020). 'Making sense of the perceptual capacities in autistic and non-autistic adults.' *Autism, 24*(7). https://doi.org/10.1177/1362361320922640

17. Rimland, B. & Fein, D. (1988). 'Special talents of autistic savants.' In L. K. Obler & D. Fein (Eds.), *The exceptional brain: neuropsychology of talent and special abilities* (pp. 472–492). Guildford Press.

18. Stanutz, S., Wapnick, J. & Burack, J. A. (2014). 'Pitch discrimination and melodic memory in children with autism spectrum disorders.' *Autism, 18*(2), 137–147. https://doi.org/10.1177/1362361312462905.
19. Davies, W. J. (2022) Autistic Listening. In J. L. Drever & Hugill, A (Eds.), *Aural Diversity.* Routledge. https://doi.org/10.4324/9781003183624-10

Chapter Three

1. Maïano, C., Normand, C. L., Salvas, M., Moullec, G. & Aimé, A. (2016). 'Prevalence of school bullying among youth with autism spectrum disorders: a systematic review and meta-analysis.' *Autism Research, 9*(6), 601–615. https://doi.org/10.1002/aur.1568.
2. 'Bullying.' *Ambitious about Autism.* (2022). https://www.ambitiousaboutautism.org.uk/information-about-autism/in-education/bullying
3. Cassidy, S., Bradley, L., Shaw, R. & Baron-Cohen, S. (2018). 'Risk markers for suicidality in autistic adults.' *Molecular Autism, 9*(42). https://doi.org/10.1186/s13229-018-0226-4
4. Kupferstein, H. (2018). 'Evidence of increased PTSD symptoms in autistics exposed to applied behavior analysis.' *Advances in Autism, 4*(1), 19–29. https://doi.org/10.1108/AIA-08-2017-0016
5. 'Why ABA therapy is harmful to autistic people.' *Autistic Science Person.* (2021). https://autisticscienceperson.com/why-aba-therapy-is-harmful-to-autistic-people/#what-research-says
6. Strydom, A., Bosco, A., Vickerstaff, V., Hunter, R. & Hassiotis, A. (2020). 'Clinical and cost effectiveness of staff training in the delivery of Positive Behaviour Support (PBS) for adults with intellectual disabilities, autism spectrum disorder and challenging behaviour – randomised trial.' *BMC Psychaitry, 20*(161). https://doi.org/10.1186/s12888-020-02577-1
7. Reichow, B., Hume, K., Barton, E. E. & Boyd, B. A. (2018). 'Early intensive behavioral intervention (EIBI) for increasing functional behaviors and skills in young children with autism spectrum disorders (ASD).' *Cochrane Database of Systematic Review, 2018*(5), Article CD009260. https://doi.org/10.1002/14651858.CD009260.pub3
8. Dai, Y. G. et al. (2022). 'An initial trial of OPT-In Early: an online training program for caregivers of autistic children.' *Autism, 0*(0). https://doi.org/10.1177/13623613221142408

9. Kupferstein, 'Evidence of increased PTSD symptoms in autistics exposed to applied behavior analysis.'

10. Cassidy et al, 'Risk markers for suicidality in autistic adults.'

11. Mandell, D. S., Ittenbach, R. F., Levy, S. E. & Pinto-Martin, J. A. (2007). 'Disparities in diagnoses received prior to a diagnosis of autism spectrum disorder.' *The Journal of Autism and Developmental Disorders, 37*(9), 1795–1802. https://doi.org/10.1007/s10803-006-0314-8

12. Price, D. (2022). *Unmasking autism: the power of embracing our hidden neurodiversity.* Monoray.

13. Abrams, A. (2020). 'Black, disabled and at risk: the overlooked problem of police violence against Americans with disabilities.' https://time.com/5857438/police-violence-black-disabled/

14. Associated Press. (2018). 'Video shows off-duty Chicago police officer shooting unarmed autistic man.' https://www.theguardian.com/us-news/2018/oct/17/video-shows-chicago-police-officer-shoot-unarmed-autistic-man

15. Phillip, R. (2022). 'Overpoliced and adultified: how the justice system is failing autistic Black people.' Gal-dem. https://gal-dem.com/overpoliced-adultified-police-failing-black-autistic-people/

16. Abdul, G. (2022, Apr 28). 'Non-verbal black teenager who has never left UK detained at immigration centre.' *The Guardian.* https://www.theguardian.com/world/2022/apr/28/non-verbal-black-teenager-who-has-never-left-uk-detained-at-immigration-centre

17. Ventour-Griffiths, T. (2022). 'Autistic while Black in the UK: masking, codeswitching, and other (non)fictions.' *Neuroclastic: the autism spectrum according to autistic people.* https://neuroclastic.com/long-read-autistic-while-black-in-the-uk-masking-codeswitching-and-other-nonfictions/

Chapter Four

1. Wood, R. (2021). 'Autism, intense interests and support in school: from wasted efforts to shared understandings.' *Educational Review, 73*(1), 34–54. https://doi.org/10.1080/00131911.2019.1566213

2. *Equality Act 2010* (c.15). https://www.legislation.gov.uk/ukpga/2010/15/contents

Chapter Five

1. Hume, K., Regan, T., Megronigle, L. & Rhinehalt, C. (2016). 'Supporting students with autism spectrum disorder through grief and loss.' *Teaching Exceptional Children, 48*(3), 128–136. https://doi.org/10.1177/0040059915618196

Chapter Six

1. Lever, A. G. & Geurts, H. M. (2016). 'Psychiatric co-occurring symptoms and disorders in young, middle-aged, and older adults with autism spectrum disorder.' *Journal of Autism and Developmental Disorders, 46*(2016), 1916–1930. https://doi.org/10.1007/s10803-016-2722-8
2. Brown, T. M. & Fee, E. (2002). 'Walter Bradford Cannon: Pioneer physiologist of human emotions.' *American Journal of Public Health, 92*(10), 1594–1595.
3. Waxenbaum, J. A., Reddy, V. & Varacallo, M. (2022). *Anatomy, Autonomic Nervous System.* StatPearls Publishing.
4. Cannon, W. B. (1915). *Bodily changes in pain, hunger, fear and rage.* D. Appleton & Company.
5. Barlow, D. H. (2002). *Anxiety and its disorders* (2nd ed.). Guildford Press.
6. Kinnaird, E., Stewart, C. & Tchanturia, K. (2019). 'Investigating alexithymia in autism: a systematic review and meta-analysis.' *European Psychiatry, 55,* 80–89. https://doi.org/10.1016/j.eurpsy.2018.09.004

Chapter Seven

1. Widnall, E. et al. (2022). 'Autism spectrum disorders as a risk factor for adolescent self-harm: a retrospective cohort study of 113,286 young people in the UK.' *BMC Medicine, 20.* https://doi.org/10.1186/s12916-022-02329-w
2. Blanchard, A., Chihuri, S. DiGuiseppi, C. G. & Li, G. (2021). 'Risk of self-harm in children and adults with autism spectrum disorder: a systematic review and meta-analysis.' *JAMA Network Open, 4*(10), Article e2130272. https://doi.org/10.1001/jamanetworkopen.2021.30272
3. The Children's Society. (2018). *The good childhood report 2018.* https://www.basw.co.uk/resources/good-childhood-report-2018
4. Marsh, S. & Boateng, A. (2018, Aug 29). 'Quarter of 14-year-old girls in UK have self-harmed, report finds.' *The*

Guardian. https://www.theguardian.com/society/2018/aug/29/ quarter-of-14-year-old-girls-in-uk-have-self-harmed-report-finds

5. Knipe, D., Padmanathan, P., Newton-Howes, G., Chan, L. F. & Kapur, N. (2022). 'Suicide and self-harm.' *The Lancet, 399*(10338), 14–20. https:// doi.org/10.1016/S0140-6736(22)00173-8

Chapter Eight

1. Van Steensel, F. J. A., Bögels, S. M. & Perrin, S. (2011). 'Anxiety disorders in children and adolescents with autistic spectrum disorders: a meta-analysis.' *Clinical Child and Family Psychology Review, 14*(3), 302–317. https://doi.org/10.1007/s10567-011-0097-0
2. OCD UK. (2022). *Occurences of OCD.* https://www.ocduk.org/ocd/ how-common-is-ocd/

Chapter Eleven

1. National Autistic Society. (2023). *Number of autistic people in mental health hospitals: latest data.* https://www.autism.org.uk/what-we-do/ news/autistic-people-in-mental-health-hospitals-latest
2. National Autistic Society. (2023). *Number of autistic people in mental health hospitals*
3. Newell, V., Phillips, L., Jones, C., Townsend, E., Richards, C. & Cassidy, S. (2023). 'A systematic review and meta-analysis of suicidality in autistic and possibly autistic people without co-occurring intellectual disability.' *Molecular Autism, 14*(1), 12. https://doi.org.10.1186/ s13229-023-00544-7.
4. Cassidy, S., Bradley, P., Robinson, J., Allison, C., McHugh, M., Baron-Cohen, S. (2014). 'Suicidal ideation and suicide plans or attempts in adults with Asperger's syndrome attending a specialist diagnosistic clinic: a clinical cohort study.' *The Lancet Psychiatry, 1*(2), 142–147. https://doi.org/10.1016/ S2215-0366(14) 70248-2
5. Richards, G. Kenny, R., Griffiths, S., Allison, C., Mosse, D., Holt, R., O'Connor, R. C., Cassidy, S. & Baron-Cohen, S. (2019). 'Autistic traits in adults who have attempted suicide.' *Molecular Autism, 10*(26). https://doi. org/10.1186/s13229-019-0274-4
6. Cassidy, S., Au-Yeung, S., Robertson, A., Cogger-Ward, H., Richards, G., Allison, C., Bradley, L., Kenny, R., O'Connor, R., Mosse, D., Rodgers, J. & Baron-Cohen, S. (2022). 'Autism and autistic traits in those

who died by suicide in England.' *The British Journal of Psychiatry, 221*(5), 683–691. https://doi.org/10.1192/bjp.2022.21

7. National Development for Inclusion. (2021). '"It's not rocket science': Considering and meeting the sensory needs of autistic children and young people in CAMHS inpatient services.' https://www.ndti.org.uk/resources/publication/its-not-rocket-science

8. Chabrol. H. (2018). 'The co-occurrence of autistic traits and borderline personality disorder is associated to increased suicidal ideation in nonclinical young adults.' *Comprehensive Psychiatry, 82,* 141–143. https://doi.org/10.1016/j.comppsych.2018.02.006

9. Dudas, R. B., Lovejoy, C., Cassidy, S., Allison, C., Smith, P. & Baron-Cohen, S. (2018). 'The overlap between autistic spectrum conditions and borderline personality disorder.' *PLOS ONE, 13*(1), Article e0190727. https://doi.org/10.1371/journal.pone.0190727

Chapter Twelve

1. Wassell, C. & Burke, E. (2022). *Autism, girls, & keeping it all inside.* Autistic Girls Network. https://autisticgirlsnetwork.org/wp-content/uploads/2022/03/Keeping-it-all-inside.pdf

2. Gould, J. & Ashton-Smith, J. (2011). 'Missed diagnosis or misdiagnosis? Girls and women on the autism spectrum.' *Good Autism Practice, 12*(1), 34–41.

3. Milner, V., McIntosh, H., Colvert, E. & Happé, F. (2019). 'A qualitative exploration of the female experience of autism spectrum disorder (ASD).' *Journal of Autism and Developmental Disorders, 49*(6), 2389–2402. https://doi.org/10.1007/s10803-019-03906-4

4. Kanner, 'Autistic disturbances of affective contact.'

5. Sheffer, E. (2018). *Asperger's children: the origins of autism in Nazi Vienna.* W. W. Norton & Company.

6. Silberman, *NeuroTribes.*

7. Baron-Cohen. (2002). 'The extreme male brain theory of autism.' *Trends in Cognitive Science, 6*(6), 248–254. https://doi.org/10.1016/s1364-6613(02)01904-6

8. Auyeung, B., Baron-Cohen, S., Ashwin, E., Knickmeyer, R., Taylor, K. & Hackett, G. (2009). 'Fetal testosterone and autistic traits.' *British Journal of Psychology, 100,* 1–22. https://doi.org/10.1348/000712608X311731

9. Wing, L. (1981). 'Sex ratios in early childhood autism and related conditions.' *Psychiatry Research, 5*(2), 129–137. https://doi.org/10.1016/0165-1781(81)90043-3

10. Hull, L., Petrides, K. V. & Mandy, W. (2020). 'The female autism phenotype and camouflaging: a narrative review.' *Review Journal of Autism and Developmental Disorders, 7,* 306–317. https://doi.org/10.1007/s40489-020-00197-9

11. Davies, S. (pre-publication) at Swansea University

12. McCrossin, 'Finding the true number of females with autistic spectrum disorder by estimating the biases in initial recognition and clinical diagnosis.'

13. Happé, F., Mansour, H., Barrett, P., Brown, T., Abbott, P., & Charlton, R. (2016). 'Demographic and cognitive profile of individuals seeking a diagnosis of autism spectrum disorder in adulthood.' *Journal of Autism and Developmental Disorders, 46*(11), 3469–3480. https://doi.org/10.1007/s10803-016-2886-2

14. Roman-Urrestarazu, A., van Kessell, R., Allison, C., Matthews, F., Brayne, C. & Baron-Cohen, S. (2021). 'Association of race/ ethnicity and social disadvantage with autism prevalence in 7 million school children in England.' *JAMA Pediatrics, 175*(6). https://doi.org/10.1001/jamapediatrics.2021.0054

15. Wassell, C. & Burke, E., *Autism, girls, & keeping it all inside.*

16. Roman-Urrestarazu, et al, 'Association of race/ ethnicity and social disadvantage with autism prevalence in 7 million school children in England.'

Chapter Thirteen

1. Loomes, R., Hull, L., Polmear, W. & Mandy, W. P. L. (2017). 'What is the male-to-female ratio in autism spectrum disorder? A systematic review and meta-analysis.' *Journal of the American Academy of Child and Adolescent Psychiatry, 56*(6), 466–474. https://doi.org/10.1016/j.jaac.2017.03.013

2. Harrison, J. L., Brownlow, C. L. Ireland, M. J. & Piovesana, A. M. (2022). 'Empathy measurement in autistic and non-autistic adults: a COSMIN systematic literature review.' *Assessment, 29*(2), 332–350. https://doi.org/10.1177/1073191120964564

3. Engelbrecht, N. (2020). 'The empathy quotient.' *Embrace Autism.* https://embrace-autism.com/empathy-quotient/

4. Zadok, E., Gordon, I., Navon, R., Rabin, S. J. & Golan, O. (2022). 'Shifts in behavioral synchrony in response to an interaction partner's distress in adolescents with and without ASD.' *Journal of Autism and Developmental Disorders, 52,* 4261–4273. https://doi.org/10.1007/s10803-021-05307-y

5. Milton, D. (2012). 'On the ontological status of autism: the "double empathy problem".' *Disability and Society, 27*(6), 883–887. https://doi.org/10.1080/09687599.2012.710008

6. Crompton, C. J., Ropar, D. Evans-Williams, C. V. M., Flynn, E. G. & Fletcher-Waston, S. (2020). 'Autistic peer-to-peer information transfer is highly effective.' *Autism, 24*(7), 1704–1712. https://doi.org/10.1177/1362361320919286

7. Autistica. 'Learning disability and autism.' https://www.autistica.org.uk/what-is-autism/signs-and-symptoms/learning-disability-and-autism

8. Donaldson, A. L. & McCoy, J. (2021). '"Everyone deserves AAC": preliminary study of the experiences of speaking autistic adults who use augmentative and alternative communication.' *Perspectives of the ASHA Special Interest gROUPS, 6*(2), 315–326. https://doi.org/10.1044/2021_PERSP-20-00220

9. Nowell et al, 'Characterization of special interests in autism spectrum disorder.'

10. American Psychiatric Association, *Diagnostic and statistical manual of mental disorders* (5th ed.).

11. Bonneh, Y. S., Levanon, Y., Dean-Pardo, O., Lossos, L. & Aldini, Y. (2011). 'Abnormal speech spectrum and increased pitch variability in young autistic children.' *Frontiers in Human Neuroscience, 4,* 237. https://doi.org/10.3389/fnhum.2010.00237

12. Cassidy, S., Hannant, P., Tavassoli, T., Allison, C., Smith, P. & Baron-Cohen, S. (2016). 'Dyspraxia and autistic traits in adults with and without autism spectrum conditions.' *Molecular Autism, 7,* Article 48. https://doi.org/10.1186/s13229-016-0112-x

Chapter Fifteen

1. Asperger, H. (1991[1944]). '"Autistic Psychopathy' in Childhood.' In U. Frith (Ed.), *Autism and Asperger Syndrome* (pp. 37–92).

Originally published as '*Die "Autistischen Psychopathen" im Kindesalter*,' *Archiv für Psychiatrie und Nervenkrankenheiten* 117(1944), 76–136.

2. Wing, 'Asperger's syndrome: a clinical account'
3. Gillberg, C. (2015). 'Lorna Wing, OBE, MD, FRCPsych formerly psychiatrist and physician, Social Psychiatry Unit, Institute of Psychiatry, King's College London, co-founder of the UK National Autistic Society.' *BJPsych Bulletin, 39*(1), 52–53. https://doi.org/10.1192/pb.bp.114.048900
4. Czech, H. (2018). 'Hans Asperger, national socialism, and "race hygiene" in Nazi-era Vienna.' *Molecular Autism, 9.* https://doi.org/10.1186/s13229-018-0208-6
5. Baron-Cohen, 'The extreme male brain theory of autism.'
6. Autistic Self Advocacy Network. (2023). 'Disability community day of mourning.' https://autisticadvocacy.org/mourning/

Chapter Sixteen

1. McVeigh, T. (2014, Jun 14). 'Half of autistic adults "abused by someone they trusted as a friend".' *The Guardian.* https://www.theguardian.com/society/2014/jun/14/autistic-adults-abused-by-friends-survey
2. Toseeb, U., McChesney, G., Oldfield, J. & Wolke, D. (2020). 'Sibling bullying in middle childhood is associated with psychosocial difficulties in early adolescence: the case of individuals with autism spectrum disorder.' *Journal of Autism and Developmental Disorders*, 50, 1457–1469. https://doi.org/10.1007/s10803-019-04116-8
3. U.S. Department of Health and Human Sciences. 'Facts about bullying.' *Stopbullying.* https://www.stopbullying.gov/resources/facts
4. Cazalis, F., Reyes, E., Leduc, S. & Gourion, D. (2022). 'Evidence that nine autistic women out of ten have been victims of sexual violence.' *Frontiers in Behavioral Neuroscience, 16,* Article 852203. https://doi.org/10.3389/fnbeh.2022.852203
5. Lever, A. G. & Geurts, H. M. (2016). 'Psychiatric co-occurring symptoms and disorders in young, middle-aged, and older adults with autism spectrum disorder.' *Journal of Autism and Developmental Disorders, 46*(2016), 1916–1930. https://doi.org/10.1007/s10803-016-2722-8
6. Autistica. 'Suicide and autism.' https://www.autistica.org.uk/what-is-autism/signs-and-symptoms/suicide-and-autism

QUOTATION CREDITS

Page 11: 'Imagination is the only weapon...' attrib. Benjamin de Casseres, 1916

Page 23: 'why else are we here...' © butterflies rising 2018, from butterfliesrising.com; copyright © 2020 'wild spirit, soft heart'; © 2022 'go where you breathe free'.

Page 37: 'As the river runs wild...' © Morgan Harper Nichols *c*.2019.

Page 51: 'I like school and I hate it...' © Jonny Heath 2020.

Page 71: 'There is no easy way...' Seneca, date unknown

Page 83: 'Without fear there cannot be...' © Christopher Paolini.

Page 99: 'Throughout it all, you are...' © Leila Sales 2013, from *This Song Will Save Your Life*.

Page 113: 'Torture: knowing something makes...' © Corey Ann Haydu 2014, from *OCD Love Story*.

Page 133: 'Sometimes, all you can do...' © William C Hannan 2015

Page 149: 'She's in the clouds...' © Christy Ann Martine 2013, from *She'll Find the Sky: A Collection of Poems* by Christy Ann Martine (2021).

Page 155: 'There comes a point...' © Ranata Suzuki 2018, from *The Longest Night: A collection of poetry from a life half-lived* (Ranata Suzuki, 2018).

Page 177: 'Do not waste time...' © Cailin Hargreaves 2023, from *Be the Light: Words to inspire gratitude, hope and happiness* (Welbeck Balance, 2023).

Page 195: 'We must be willing to...' Joseph Campbell, quoted in *Reflections on the Art of Living: A Joseph Campbell Companion* by Diane Osbon (Harper Perennial, 1995)

Page 209: 'By being yourself you...' Edwin Elliott.

Page 217: 'The problem was never...' © Shannon L Alder.

Page 235: 'Sometimes you have to...' Emma Xu, discovered via https://www.ourmindfullife.com/vulnerability-quotes/

Page 247: 'You are not your past...' © Shannon L Alder.

ACKNOWLEDGEMENTS

This book wouldn't exist, nor would I be where I am today, without the love, support and guidance of those who made it possible.

To Mum and Dad. I cannot possibly list all the things I am thankful to you for. You made sure I knew what it felt like to be loved and you have always been a constant in a world full of change. Without you, the ending of this book would have been a very different one.

Thomas and Jessica. Thank you for going along with my wild imagination and spending hours upon end in the world of Crystal Kingdom. The fun memories of our childhood will never not outweigh the bickering. I promise I will not make you write your own novels or diaries again.

Coco – the best four-legged friend I could have ever asked for. And a wonderful writing companion. Thank you for making me smile on my darkest days and for motivating me to get better and out of hospital. You made my world from the age of 15 to 22 a much brighter place. I will miss you forever.

Grannie and Grandpa – thank you for your never-ending encouragement of my writing endeavours and for all the holidays to Hope Cove. And Grandma and Grandad – thank you for all the love and support from the other side of the world. I know Grandpa and Grandad would be proud of me.

And of course, to Connor. Thank you for coming into my life when I was 19, for loving the unmasked me, and for learning as much as you could about autism overnight.

Your reassurance throughout this book process has not gone unnoticed!

To Elouise, Maya and Chloe – thank you for making school more bearable, for choosing takeaways over restaurants so I could join in, and for making me smile every day for seven years. I am so glad my teenage years were spent with you – girls who chose acceptance and love over drama every single time. From the age of 11 till now, you have always been the first people I want to call when I need to smile.

To Lauren, Katie and Jenny – thank you for being the light in the worst three months of my life and being the only people who understand exactly what that time was like. It was less lonely because of you.

I am deeply grateful for the influence of several special teachers who never faltered in their support of me. Mrs Girdwood, my Year 6 teacher, for knowing that I would be an author one day and encouraging me in every way possible. My English teachers, Miss Bliss and Ms Absalom, who were the kind of teachers that made school feel like a safe place. Mrs Zanetti, who made reintegrating into sixth form and sitting my A-levels possible. Miss Wood, for giving me a space to regulate and helping me to understand myself. And the various librarians over the years – for providing a haven for me even when the library was meant to be shut.

And to the professionals who are gems within the mental health system – in-particular to Luca and Sarah, who never made assumptions about me based on a diagnosis, gave me the time I needed to build trust, and valued my insight and knowledge. Thank you for going above and beyond for me and helping me learn tools to cope.

Thank you to everyone at Octopus Publishing Group who helped *Girl Unmasked* become what it is. A very special thank you to Jake Lingwood, for seeing what the messy first draft could be and for helping it to get there, to Mel Four for the beautiful cover design, and to Pauline Bache, whose talent in the editorial process (and patience with my perfectionism!) is greatly appreciated. And thank you to Andrew Chapman from ID Audio for making recording the audiobook a lot more fun and less anxiety-inducing than it could have been.

To my brilliant agent, Jessica Killingley, and The BKS Agency – your instant belief in my writing and your insistence that my story was worth telling gave me the courage I needed to persevere. Thank you for your guidance every step of the way.

It is thanks to Cathy Wassell, the truly amazing CEO of Autistic Girls Network, that Jessica and I met. And thank you for inviting me to be a trustee of this incredibly important charity. It is a pleasure and a privilege.

I am indebted to everyone who has provided me with advice along this journey. Particularly to the autistic authors I look up to and whose words and worlds have provided me with much-needed comfort - Elle McNicoll, Sara Gibbs, Pete Wharmby, Holly Smale and Fern Brady, to name a few.

And finally, thank you to the autistic community. For welcoming 16-year-old me and showing me that I was not alone. To those who have been in this space for years longer than I have – thank you for your tireless work, advocacy and sharing of your experiences. It is from you that I learned everything that I know. And to those who follow along my journey – I am deeply grateful; your support is the reason this book exists.

ABOUT THE AUTHOR

Emily Katy, 22, lived as an undiagnosed autistic girl for nearly 17 years.

After completing her degree in 2022, she qualified as a mental health nurse. She has a large, highly engaged following on X (formerly Twitter) and Instagram (@ItsEmilyKaty) and a blog www.authenticallyemily.uk, where she talks about autism, ADHD and mental health.

Emily is a Trustee of the charity, The Autistic Girls Network, and in 2021 she was selected by the Women of the World Foundation as one of their 40 Young Leaders.

She lives in Hertfordshire with her family and her dog, and loves books, writing, scrapbooking and *Grey's Anatomy*.

This is her first book.